Ross Macdonald

**RECOGNITIONS**

detective/suspense · science fiction

Dick Riley, General Editor

# Ross Macdonald

## BY JERRY SPEIR

Frederick Ungar Publishing Co. / New York

*To Barbara*

Copyright © 1978 by Frederick Ungar Publishing Co., Inc.
Printed in the United States of America
Designed by Patrick Vitacco

**Library of Congress Cataloging in Publication Data**

Speir, Jerry, 1946–
    Ross Macdonald.

    (Recognitions)
    Bibliography: p.
    1. Millar, Kenneth, 1915–    —Criticism and interpretation.
2. Detective and mystery stories, American—History and criticism.
PS3525.I486Z87        813'.5'2        78-4297
ISBN 0-8044-2824-7
ISBN 0-8044-6871-0 pbk.

# Contents

The evil that men do lives after them.
*Julius Caesar* (Shakespeare)

# Clues to the Reader

Detective novels are by their very nature a kind of puzzle. One begins reading a detective mystery with the assumption that there is a puzzle to be figured out—the puzzle of the crime. Who did it? And why? Too often readers and critics confine their analyses to how well individual novels succeed as puzzles and completely disregard the larger structure of the writer's entire body of work. Macdonald, as I hope these pages demonstrate, has a much larger purpose than the construction of individual games for intellectual distraction. He analyzes contemporary society and the shaky psychological substructure on which it rests. Frequently his plots reflect classical mythology twisted or distorted by modern circumstances to reveal a new mythology, one depicting California as the symbol of man's inability to cope with himself, his fellow man, and the world. This book makes a first attempt at exposing this over-all unity behind Macdonald's work and acknowledges the expanses still open to interpretation.

Some comments on the peculiarities of such a study appear necessary. First, it should be scrupulously noted that plot summaries of stories as tightly constructed as Macdonald's are impossible to provide without either omitting substantial subplots or recapitulating the entire story paragraph by paragraph. The summaries that appear here tend to take what I see as either the major theme of a book or the feature most obviously distinguishing it from the other novels and to follow that single idea through the plot. There is no substitute for enjoying the books themselves. I should also cau-

tion the reader that certain plots are "given away" in these
pages. Since the final twist is one of a detective novel's
singular attributes, I have tried to limit these revelations.
But trying to interpret Macdonald without discussing endings would be a bit like trying to analyze Shakespeare without revealing his last acts. Endings complete a novel's structure, and that structure is virtually meaningless without
them. So be warned. The endings of *The Doomsters, The
Galton Case, The Zebra-Striped Hearse, Black Money, The
Goodbye Look,* and *The Underground Man* are all discussed
here in detail. And to a lesser extent, the resolutions of *The
Three Roads* and *The Blue Hammer* are also revealed.

A note on the organization and intended use of this book
may also be in order. Chapter 1 is a brief biography of the
author and includes some of Macdonald's own thoughts on
his work. Since Macdonald is a pseudonym, the author is
referred to only in this chapter as Kenneth Millar in order
to avoid some awkward constructions. Chapters 2 to 4 examine the novels individually and in the order of their writing. Though each is treated in its own terms, the development of central themes from book to book is a primary
concern. Chapter 5 distills the personal information avail-
able about Archer from all the books and draws conclusions
about his function in the development of Macdonald's major
ideas. Chapter 6 chronicles the author's preoccupation with
alienation and related themes throughout the novels. Chapter 7 makes a brief statement on the author's style, and the
final chapter considers the limited scholarly criticism directed toward the genre and Macdonald while attempting
a preliminary evaluation of his literary worth.

This organization will allow for many possible uses. The
reader thoroughly familiar with the novels may want to
skip first to Chapter 6 and look into general themes—though
he will have missed the development of numerous minor
themes in Chapters 2 to 4. Or a reader who knows only some
of the novels may want to concentrate on those and skip the
interpretations of others he has not yet read, saving the
pleasure of discovery for the novels themselves. A teacher
using this book as a supplement for a course in popular

fiction might wish to take advantage of the relative independence of chapters in making assignments. And, it is hoped, the bibliography will aid students and future critics in locating the materials that bear directly on any study of Macdonald.

A final note on mechanics. Footnotes for all references, quotations from the novels included, follow the final chapter and are identified by page numbers and the last three words of the quote. No superscript numbers are included in the text.

This book could not have been completed without considerable assistance. My greatest debt is to Kenneth Millar—for writing such a fine series of books and for agreeing to talk to me about them. To my good friend Dr. Barbara Ewell, I am indebted for assistance in every phase from formulation of ideas through rewriting and proofreading. To my friend Dr. Michael Zimmerman I am grateful for many hours of conversation that helped form the philosophical background of my interpretations. To my friends and fellow Macdonald enthusiasts Dr. Edward Murphy and Donald McNabb, I owe many thanks for time spent comparing ideas on the novels. And to my editor, Dick Riley, I owe appreciation for his patience and encouragement.

J.S.

New Orleans
June 1978

# 1

# The Writer in Disguise

> Disguise is the imaginative device which
> permits the work to be both private and
> public, to half-divulge the writer's crucial
> secrets while deepening the whole com-
> munity's sense of its own mysterious life.
> "Writing *The Galton Case*"

Ross Macdonald is the pseudonym of Kenneth Millar. Since the world of his novels is largely, and admittedly, autobiographical, any real comprehension of this world demands attention to the details of his life.

Kenneth Millar was born in Los Gatos, California, near San Francisco, on December 13, 1915. Shortly afterward his family moved to Vancouver, British Columbia; Millar spent his entire boyhood, adolescence, and early adulthood in Canada. He did not return to the United States until 1938, when he attended summer school at the University of Michigan, and his experience as a man of two countries has had a profound effect on his later life and the world of his fiction. *The Galton Case* (1959), his thirteenth novel, traces the life of a young man born in California, reared in Canada, and finally returned to California via Michigan in what Millar has called "a story roughly shaped on my own early life, transformed and simplified into a kind of legend." All his fiction can be read as an attempt to capture the essence of the contemporary world through the transforming, distorting lens of personal experience, and it is that lens which is the subject here.

Millar has said that he "was born with a fatal predisposition to words," alluding to his journalist father and grandfather and to writers also on his mother's side of the family. An early recollection is of Saturday afternoon serials at the

1

local movie house viewing such episodes as Pearl White's "Plunder," and he recalls of these exposures to melodrama that "The terrors with which the episodes ended, the satisfactions with which they began, left a permanent impression on my nerves." His fictional detective, Lew Archer, remembers a similar influence in childhood, but this simple incident of transference of a bit of his own life to the fictional backgrounds of his characters is only a minor example of the kind of mixing of fact and fiction that is the basis and strength of Millar's art.

Millar's earliest recorded memory is of his father. As well as a journalist, his father was for a time a harbor pilot in Vancouver, and Millar recalls a day in 1919 (when he would have been only three years old), when "my sea-captain father took me on a brief voyage and showed me a shining oceanic world from which I ha[ve] felt exiled ever since, even during my sea duty in the Navy." Bound up in that memory are two powerful influences on his writings: his father and the sea.

Shortly after that brief voyage with his father, Millar's parents separated and he entered a long period of frequent relocation (sometimes with and sometimes without his partially invalid mother), living first with one relative and then with another, a phase that did not end until his graduation from high school in 1932. At that time, he says, "I counted the rooms I had lived in during my first sixteen years, and got a total of fifty." The separation from his father and Millar's subsequent search for identity, for continuity in a disjointed existence, marked his fiction as well as his life. Many of the fictional characters of his mature work are absorbed in such a quest. Particularly since his breakthrough in *The Doomsters* (1958) and, more significantly, in *The Galton Case* (1959), the family saga has provided him a form for dealing with this explosive, autobiographical material.

An important aspect of that later work is the author's use of the sea and of water imagery in general (see Chapter 6). The symbol is obviously bound up with recollections of his father and his own father-search. Millar has called the sea "the most important physical thing in my life," and still swims almost daily in the Pacific near his Santa Barbara home. His father was a swimming champion, and Millar is himself an excellent swimmer, having been a tower diver in his younger years. As the novels develop, the sea becomes an external image for expressing freedom, openness, and a union with the powerful forces of nature. It also becomes an internal image for suggesting all the psychologically submerged horror passed from generation to generation without codification, explanation, or even acknowledgment.

In the course of Millar's youthful wanderings, he spent two years, from about age twelve, in a boarding school, St. John's, in Winnipeg. During that time he began his writing career, turning out "a sheaf of western stories and a long narrative poem about Bonnie Prince Charlie." Since his grandfather was from Scotland, and Prince Charlie and the Stuarts were its lost kings, the subject seemed appropriate. Already, Millar was "searching for a tradition that would relate to my life and the place."

The economic crash of 1929 was the next major force in the young writer's life. It forced him out of the Winnipeg school where a father's sister had been paying tuition and put him down in Medicine Hat, Alberta, for a year with one of his mother's sisters. Following that he returned to the maternal family home in Kitchener, Ontario, where he lived with his mother and grandmother until he graduated from high school, the Kitchener-Waterloo Collegiate Institute, in 1932. A fellow student in his homeroom class and on the same debating team was a girl by the name of Margaret Sturm. Millar was not to see her again until six years after their graduation, but she subsequently became his wife, well known as the novelist Margaret Millar. Coincidentally, both their first published stories appeared in the same issue of their high school magazine, *The Grumbler*. Millar's story, prophetically, was a parody of Conan Doyle, called "The South Sea Soup Co." which began

> The ambitious young investigator, Herlock Sholmes, yawned behind his false mustache and poured for himself a cocaine-and-soda.

Other literary influences from this adolescent period, be-
sides Conan Doyle, were Dostoevsky, the *Black Mask* magazine for which Chandler and Hammett wrote, and Stephen
Leacock, the dominant Canadian prose stylist of the time.

Having graduated from high school during the Great
Depression in 1932, Millar found himself "glad to work on a
farm for my board alone." Though the year on the farm
agreed with his health, it also stirred in him a new class
consciousness. Like many others, he discovered the "moral
pain inflicted . . . by the doctrine . . . that poverty is always
deserved." And his dilemma was deepened, as he says,

> by my fear that I'd never make it to college, and by my feeling
> of exile, which my mother had cultivated by teaching me from
> early childhood that California was my birthplace and natural
> home.

But, though he continued to work on the farm during the
summers, he did manage to attend college at the University
of Western Ontario. Between his junior and senior years
there, he took a year off, partially prompted by the death of
his mother, and traveled to Europe. He passed his twenty-
first birthday abroad. The time was 1936–37. Following a
cycling trip through the British Isles and France, he made
his way to Germany where he witnessed first-hand the pre-
war Nazi build-up—an experience that later served as the
backdrop for his first novel, *The Dark Tunnel*. In that book
he made use of an experience in Germany that serves as a
central image of the place and time. While standing along
a parade route to get a glimpse of Hitler marching by to the
Horst Wessel song, Millar had his pipe knocked from his
mouth by someone who considered smoking disrespectful to
the Führer and the anthem. That incident and the general
atmosphere of the time started him on his journey home.

Shortly after his return, a fortunate coincidence altered
his life. As he has described it, "I walked into the public
library [in London, Ontario] and found Margaret reading
Thucydides in Greek. From then on, we saw each other
nearly every day." Kenneth Millar and Margaret Sturm

were married on June 2, 1938, the day after he graduated with honors from college. They spent their honeymoon in summer school at the University of Michigan in Ann Arbor. In the fall they moved to the University of Toronto, and Millar began to prepare himself to teach high school. In the spring of 1939 he "became at the same time the father of a daughter and a professional writing for money." The daughter was named Linda. The publication that first paid Millar for his writings was a Toronto weekly called *Saturday Night* to which he submitted verses, humorous sketches, and "my first few realistic stories." He was recompensed at the rate of a penny a word, but has reported that "the early joys of authorship were almost as sweet as sex."

Over the next two years, Millar taught English and history at his and his wife's old high school during the academic year and returned to do graduate work at Ann Arbor in the summers. Margaret, meanwhile, turned to writing mystery novels. Her first book, *The Invisible Worm*, was published in 1941, and it was largely her success that allowed Millar to leave high school teaching and accept a full-time fellowship at the University of Michigan in the same year. Her achievement and influence were also important in steering Millar toward the mystery genre.

Millar's own first novel, *The Dark Tunnel*, was written in Ann Arbor in the fall of 1943, but by the time it was published he had been inducted into Navy Officer Candidate School at Princeton. His second book, *Trouble Follows Me*, was written aboard an escort carrier in the Pacific. Millar served as communications officer on the ship and participated in the battle for Okinawa. That battle surfaces on more than one occasion as a significant event in Archer's past, and escort carriers are involved in the plots of several of Millar's novels. As he has commented:

> The war had a great deal to do with my becoming a professional writer. It plucked me out of graduate school, gave me a rough, short course in American geography and society, and sent me back to my native California. . . . In a way it gave me matter for all my books. Crime . . . is often war continued by other means.

Lt.(j.g.) Millar's life completed its symbolic circle in March of 1946 when he returned to California to settle in Santa Barbara, where his wife and daughter had moved during his Navy tour. That story deserves repeating. Since Millar was initially to be shipped out of San Diego, his wife and daughter had followed him there. After his departure, Margaret and Linda were on their way back to Ontario by train when Margaret first saw Santa Barbara out the window and fell in love. The train reached San Luis Obispo before they could disembark and head back south. Millar thus returned from the war to a home he had never seen in the state where he was born but which he had left at a very early age. With only brief exceptions, he has been settled there ever since.

Between his return from the service in March and the end of 1946, he finished two more novels, *Blue City* and *The Three Roads*, "in a kind of angry rapture," while writing in an overcoat and shivering through a chilly winter in a four-room stucco house with orange trees in the backyard but no effective heating. But the next year wasn't so fortunate. Feeling obliged to record his rather bleak Canadian childhood, he set about writing an autobiographical novel. The effort was not satisfying, and Millar even began to doubt his vocation as writer. As he puts it, "I was in trouble, and Lew Archer got me out of it."

The first Archer novel, *The Moving Target*, appeared in 1949. Millar credits Archer with interposing a shield, "like protective lead, between me and the radioactive material" of his experience. The novels have appeared regularly (twenty-four through 1978) ever since. It was also in this period that Millar developed his pseudonym. His original motivation was to avoid confusion and competition with his wife, Margaret Millar, who had published nine novels through 1949.

At first I called myself John Macdonald, which came from my father's name, John Macdonald Millar. But that same year, John D. MacDonald came out with a book, and his mother bought ten copies of mine by mistake. Next I tried John Ross

Macdonald. The Ross came from nowhere. It's just a common Canadian name, but it stuck, and I dropped the John.

But even as he continued to produce mystery novels under his new name, Millar maintained his interest in finishing graduate school. Between 1948 and 1951 he completed the requirements for the Ph.D. at the University of Michigan. He was awarded the degree in 1951 for a dissertation entitled, "The Inward Eye: A Revaluation of Coleridge's Psychological Criticism." The work derives from Coleridge's criticism a "psychological theory of poetic" and places that theory in both a Continental and an English perspective. It comprises a history of ideas on the subject of mind and matter. But *The Three Roads* (1948) had already signalled the author's abiding interest in psychology. The massive effort of reviewing the history of philosophical psychology that went into the dissertation obviously suggests a source of the psychological framework of subsequent novels. But Millar has also acknowledged a debt to more modern psychologists, "to Freud and all his disciples." He credits Freud with having "deepened our moral vision and rendered it forever ambivalent." Freud, he says,

> was one of the two or three great influences on me. He made myth into psychiatry, and I've been trying to turn it back into myth again in my own small way.

The extent to which Millar succeeds in turning psychiatry into myth is the subject of much of this book.

But the man Millar has called "the most important single influence on my life" is W. H. Auden. Auden, the English-born American poet, critic, and playwright was on the faculty at the University of Michigan during Millar's tenure there. Millar studied Modern European Literature under Auden, a subject that was taken to cover "Dante to Kafka." But more importantly, Auden had his own self-confessed addiction to detective stories and was, in fact, writing reviews of detective/mystery/crime novels for London newspapers while he was at Michigan. He encouraged both

Kenneth and Margaret Millar in the genre, which Auden believed capable of considerable literary importance and power. Millar referred to Auden as "one of the most complete minds I've ever met with." For a man of such stature to encourage a young novelist in a pursuit often considered frivolous was surely an important factor in shaping Millar's final choice of genre.

After his wife, Auden, Freud, and perhaps Coleridge, Dostoevsky must rank as a principal influence on the writer's work. Millar was reading Dostoevsky even as a teenager. When questioned about whether the title *The Underground Man* was in deliberate reference to Dostoevsky (*Notes from Underground*), Millar responded, "Actually, a lot of my *thinking* is in reference to Dostoevsky." The typically Dostoevskian themes of crime, guilt, and suffering are evident throughout Millar's novels (see Chapter 6). Especially in the later works, the discovery of universal guilt and the analysis of various characters' adjustment to it constitute a dominant motif.

The list of other influences on Millar is long and varied. Among detective writers, the primary models are Dashiell Hammett and Raymond Chandler. He credits Hammett with being "the first American writer to use the detective story for the purposes of a major novelist, to present a vision, blazing if disenchanted, of our lives." Of Chandler, he has said, "He wrote like a slumming angel, and invested the sun-blinded streets of Los Angeles with a romantic presence." He has claimed that "Hammett and Stephen Crane taught me the modern American style based on the speaking voice." He was strongly influenced by Poe and the entire Gothic tradition descended through him from Ann Radcliffe. The highly symbolic nature of his prose can be attributed, at least partially, to schooling in Symbolist poets like Mallarmé. His books are rife with allusions to literary figures from James Fenimore Cooper to Samuel Beckett, from Dante and Shakespeare to J. D. Salinger. Among writers he admires are Faulkner, Fitzgerald, Nelson Algren, Donald Davie, Hemingway, Flannery O'Connor, Flaubert, France, Yeats, Wilkie Collins, and Eudora Welty—to give only a

partial list. When pressed to single out one, he has called
Proust his favorite author. And he "once made a case for
the theory . . . that much of the modern development of the
detective story stems from Baudelaire, his 'dandyism' and
his vision of the city as inferno."

Following receipt of his Ph.D., Millar continued to write
novels from his base in Santa Barbara. For about a year,
during the period 1956–57, he suffered through personal
experiences which he has preferred to elaborate only as
"seismic disturbances . . . in my life." The distress of that
period caused him to move with his family to the San Francisco Bay area and to undergo a period of psychotherapy as
he attempted to comprehend the peculiar shape of his own
varied life. He credits that experience with marking the
difference between his early and later works and with
freeing him to deal fictionally with the volatile material of
his own past. He began to write *The Galton Case* after returning to Santa Barbara in the summer of 1957.

Another project of that period was the teaching of creative writing in an adult education program in Santa Barbara. In 1958 and 1959 he also undertook the writing of book
reviews for *The San Francisco Chronicle*. Not surprisingly,
the more than two dozen reviews covered a wide range of
topics from psychiatry and literary criticism to biography,
fiction, and criticism of the detective novel.

In more recent years, environmental issues have occupied
a portion of his time. He is a member of the Sierra Club, the
National Audubon Society, and the American Civil Liberties
Union. In 1964 he published an article in *Sports Illustrated*
on the detrimental effects of building a road through the
Sisquoc Condor Sanctuary. One of California's raging forest
fires very nearly destroyed his home, and his environmental
concerns were turned to that problem. The incident provided material for the catastrophic story built around a fire
in *The Underground Man* (1971). In 1969 a massive oil spill
off the coast of Santa Barbara drew Millar both to the picket
lines and to organized action. With biographer/historian
Robert Easton, Millar became a co-founder of *Santa Barbara Citizens for Environmental Defense* and, subsequently,

one of the fifteen co-plaintiffs in an ACLU suit against the parties responsible for the spill. The oil spill ultimately became the organizing idea behind *Sleeping Beauty* (1973).

Increasingly, Millar's concerns have turned to the fragile relationship between the individual and technology in the contemporary world. He sees Archer as representing

> modern man in a technological society, who is, in effect, homeless, virtually friendless, and who tries to behave as if there is some hope in society, which there is.

He finds that hope in people and the relationships between them which serve as the stabilizing force in a world in transition. California is, for Millar, the microcosm of that transition. It is the place where

> it was possible for the new world to create itself. . . . That's what I'm writing about. Instead of a traditional structure holding things together, you have each man holding his own gyroscope. Technology is sweeping away all meaningful relationships and replacing them with apparatus. We have to learn to live with this loss of relationship and humanize it.

> The essential problem . . . is how you are going to maintain values, and express values in your actions, when the values aren't there in the society around you, as they are in traditional societies. In a sense, you have to make yourself up as you go along.

If the essential problem is maintaining and expressing value, the essential obstacle to a resolution of that problem is evil. Millar considers evil the subject of all crime/mystery fiction. And he sees

> the roots of the mystery novel go[ing] back to the medieval fabliau, which deliberately dealt with taboo subjects. I think it's significant that very early dramas were known as mysteries. They dealt in a more human way than the Scriptures or church services with sacred subjects and matters of good and evil. Now, of course, what used to be taboo is more or less

taken for granted. But a certain aura of evil hangs around the form.

Millar, then, sees himself as writing within an age-old, popular tradition whose purpose is the enlightenment of the masses concerning the recurrent themes of good and evil. He takes as his primary locale California, that thin band of coast at the very rim of the continent where the American Dream must be finally enacted or found lacking. In its idyllic, raw beauty between soaring mountains and shimmering ocean, man has come to the end of the West and is turned back upon himself for realization of his dreams. The profound psychological repercussions of this period of sociological and technological upheaval are reflected in Millar's novels. And he frequently speaks of his purpose in writing as didactic. He has said:

> The essence of popular art, I think, originates in the writer's desire to reach a public and take it with him.

> I have a very strong feeling that it's the duty of a writer, or at least of this particular writer, to write popular fiction. Ideally a community tends to communicate with itself through its fiction, and this communication tends to break down if there are Mandarin novels written for Mandarins and lowbrow novels written for lowbrows, and so on. My aim from the beginning has been to write novels that can be read by all kinds of people.

And throughout his attempt to restore communication on basic issues to a fragmented society, Millar's novels are informed by the history of his own fragmented life.

Another important fact of that life which has heavily influenced his writing is his sense of a double nationality—being simultaneously a product of two cultures but totally immersed in neither. He has called himself "both literally and imaginatively a biped, resting one uneasy foot in California ... and the other foot in Canada." And he has acknowledged a feeling that

Just beyond the mountains [of California] which form the
other horizon of my world, Canada seems to hang like a glacier
slowly moving down on me from its notch. I expect it to over-
take me before I die, reminding me with its chill and weight
that I belong to the north after all.

That sense of dislocation, of being an outsider, is reflected
in Archer's character and in his drive to be at once involved
and skeptical. And that unique perspective, combined with
the author's special talent and far-ranging experience and
education, is responsible for a series of books unparalleled
in American crime fiction.

# On the Way to Lew Archer

## An Examination of the Early Novels

> War and inflation always raise up a crop
> of stinkers, and a lot of them have settled
> in California.
>
> *The Moving Target*

Eleven novels precede what critics, and Ross Macdonald himself, have called the breakthroughs of *The Doomsters* (1958) and *The Galton Case* (1959). These eleven are here arbitrarily grouped as "the early novels." Through their progression, all the themes and devices that enhance the more mature fiction are meticulously developed. And, after four efforts without him, Macdonald creates Lew Archer, who gradually achieves his own seasoned character and distinct style. A chronological review of the novels shows the author experimenting with subject matter, character, atmosphere, and style. And one can perceive, in the differing approaches taken to evil, decadence, and the psychology behind them, the maturing of principal concerns of all the novels, first to last. To call Macdonald's later works more mature is not to say that these are weak; *The Three Roads* is still one of his best books on psychological matters and *Meet Me at the Morgue* boasts some of his finer plotting. But, as with most novelists, the practice of the earlier works makes for the perfection of the later. And a study of the progression of those earlier works can make for a greater appreciation of the latter.

Ross Macdonald's first novel, *The Dark Tunnel* (1944), reflects numerous autobiographical details. The central character, Robert Branch, is a young Ph.D. in English at Mid-

13

western University. Much of the novel is set in Michigan, with a trip to northern Canada structuring the climactic scenes. The plot originates in Germany, where Branch, like Macdonald, was traveling six years before.

Branch's two confrontations with Nazis during his visit establish the political context of the novel. In the first incident, he had a pipe knocked from his mouth for the impropriety of smoking in the presence of the Führer during a street demonstration. In the second, he was beaten and ultimately deported for his friendship with a Jew. Evil, in this first book, is the monolithic evil of the state, of Nazi Germany. The subject is black and white; Peter Schneider, the organizing force behind the enemy's plot, is described as "a hundred percent Aryan superman with bells on." As Macdonald's work matures, the treatment of the subject of evil grows perceptibly more ambiguous and less political. Macdonald's concerns shift steadily to the more personal, psychological roots of evil and toward the family, rather than the state as context. But it is instructive to trace that development from this initial treatment.

In the present time of the novel, 1943, Branch is a member of the War Board at the University. The Board is concerned about intelligence leaks in the University's sensitive training programs. Branch's friend and fellow War Board member, Alec Judd, dies mysteriously in an apparent suicide. By dramatic coincidence, Branch's romantic interest from his German travels, Ruth Esch, appears about to arrive at Midwestern to join the faculty. The question becomes whether she is a part of the apparent enemy plot.

The story relies on the basic chase scene and Gothic atmosphere for much of its suspense. A major part of the chase sequences take place underground in the dark service tunnels that form a labyrinth beneath the university. The subsurface setting is a first attempt at dealing figuratively with the subsurface terrors both of the individual and the society; water imagery will carry that metaphorical load in later works. On the composition of this book, Macdonald has remarked:

My first novel was written in Ann Arbor in the fall of 1943. I worked on it at night in one of the offices of the main classroom building, and the book preserves some of the atmosphere of that empty, echoing pile.

The subterranean, Gothic terror of the book is maintained even as the chase proceeds into the countryside. Branch's pursuers appear close on his heels at every new turn, despite the fact that he is going cross-country on foot and they are in an automobile on the roads. Though the device may not meet the purist's test of plausibility, it does serve to heighten the psychological alarm in the sequence and evokes considerable empathy for the very human-sized, somewhat naive protagonist ensnared in a web of overpowering evil.

The book is significant for being the place of the author's initial formulation of basic ideas. Alec Judd comments in the first chapter on what he sees in contemporary Detroit: "Grey streets bounded by grey walls. Men caught in machines. The carnivores creep between the walls on rubber tires. . . . A new kind of jungle." The alienating character of twentieth century urban, industrial life plays a progressively important role in the novels. At another point, Macdonald has Ruth Esch, Branch's German girlfriend, say:

you Americans have a certain blue-eyed look. It's not immaturity, exactly. A kind of naivete, I suppose, as if the world weren't such a bad place after all. . . . As if a single man could cope with any difficulty, and fists were effective weapons.

The comment foreshadows a primary concern of the later California novels. An overpowering belief in the sanctity of individual freedom and individual action is a motivating force in much of American fiction, with *Huckleberry Finn* as a paradigm. It is essentially an innocent idea, a belief that artificially separates the individual from the human community. Such innocence very nearly gets Robert Branch killed in *The Dark Tunnel;* and in the later novels, it is responsible for much of the familial, psychological, and social disintegration.

By the end of this book, Branch has time and reason to muse about his and others' minuscule place in the cosmos. He lies in bed looking out the window and contemplates the vast motions of the universe necessary

> to make the sun move down my blind a foot in an hour.... I thought of the inevitable past.... In the nightmare sequence of events that had seemed to grow out of each other, meaninglessly and malignantly, like cancer cells, I saw the push of giant uncontrollable forces on weak men.

This naturalistic world view is characteristic of the early novels. As the works progress, it is less obviously stated, but the influence of such naturalists as Norris, Dreiser, and Crane is persistent. Though the later works concern themselves increasingly with the degree to which personal responsibility can affect the world, the dichotomy between "giant uncontrollable forces" and "weak men" remains.

The second novel, *Trouble Follows Me* (1946), shifts the setting to Honolulu with trips to Detroit, California, Mexico and a cross-country train ride. For this plot, Macdonald draws more extensively on his military than his academic background, but, like *The Dark Tunnel*, it is primarily a novel of wartime espionage.

A brief passage in the first chapter of the novel offers a new articulation for the theme of alienation and connects it with the war itself. At a party, Sam Drake, the narrator, invites Mary Thompson, a disc jockey for the military radio station, out onto the veranda for a talk. Mary comments in the course of the conversation:

> A lot of servicemen away from home have lost track of themselves.... It's true of all of us, I guess. Not just servicemen. There aren't many people I know that haven't lost track of themselves.

Drake considers his own sense of dislocation and ponders:

"Sometimes I felt that all of us were adrift on a starless night, singing in the dark, full of fears and laughing them off with laughter which didn't fool anyone." Dislocation from a sense of place and self describes a primary affliction of the modern world. Macdonald's ever-present concern for the subject is admittedly bound up with his own sense of a dual Canadian-American nature and with the wandering life-style of his first thirty years. But the concern is not strictly personal. It is an aspect of the basic theme of alienation which will be shown to be the flaw in the paradise of California in the later works.

World War II is frequently portrayed as one of the primal forces behind that alienation. The war reshaped the sensibilities of a generation, of an age, and looms up from the past to enforce its indelible impression upon the modern world and the modern mind. Even after the novels move away from the war as an immediate backdrop, one or more of the characters with fears and motivations rooted in the era continue to haunt the books.

The sense of loss, of losing track of one's self, of being literally and psychologically adrift, serves as the basic theme for Macdonald's next two novels, *Blue City* (1947) and *The Three Roads* (1948). Characters come home after the war to confront themselves and a new world in the post-war age. The dark fears which are more easily suppressed by the pressures of war rise inexorably to the surface when that conflict is over and the participants must return home to pick up the thread of their lives in "the real world."

In *Blue City*, the pressures and fears boil over into Macdonald's most violent novel. John Weather is a young man returning to his hometown in the Midwest with hopes of reconciling himself with his father. He discovers that his father was murdered two years earlier, that his father had remarried a woman Weather has never met and that she appears to be associated with the local crime boss in operating a gambling-prostitution-drug ring. Weather is an uncontrollable, one-man vigilante squad whose wild confrontations with the Establishment (both established law and established hoodlums) are as unpredictable as the weather itself.

Corruption is pervasive in the novel, spilling over from individuals into the city itself. On seeing the city again for the first time, Weather muses:

> The city started sooner than I expected.... covering new farms with the concrete squares of suburban developments. On both sides of the highway I could see the rows of little frame houses, all alike, as if there were only one architect in the city and he had a magnificent obsession.... I caught a whiff of the rubber factories on the south side, corrupting the spring night like an armpit odor.

Reminiscent of the "new kind of jungle" of Detroit delineated in *The Dark Tunnel*, this description only thinly veils Macdonald's theme of class conflict. The antagonistic relationship between the propertied and the workers is at the root of many contemporary social ills and is given considerable treatment here only to be expanded in later novels. There, Archer can be found typically in two types of neighborhoods: the hilltop mansions of the very rich or the sealevel slums and fleabag motels of the workers and the dispossessed.

The spokesman for the propertied in this book is Alonzo Sanford, the owner of the rubber factory and numerous other local businesses. He lives in a rambling house to which "a grandiose and useless tower at each end of the facade gave ... a feudal touch." He is found reading Thorstein Veblen's *The Theory of the Leisure Class* because, as he says, "Veblen analyzes some of the illusions of my class very competently" and "helps me to be without illusions." Such descriptions are heavily ironic. The primary illusion that Veblen does not help Sanford to dispel is that the motives behind his business dealings are essentially pure. Sanford would like to believe that his is simply a small industry among giant competitors striving to keep his plant alive so that people will have jobs. If he can't pay union wages, or if he must keep his heavy hand on city government in order to keep his assessments and taxes down, he is only doing it for the good of the people of the city. Apparently, innocence is not a quality confined to veterans of the war; it extends to the molders of an oppresive economic system as well.

Weather has his own assessment of Sanford's motives: "Isn't it possible ... that you're an anachronism? You're trying to stay on top of the heap by forcing conditions to remain as you determined them fifty years ago."

Enforcing the maintenance of the *status quo* symbolizes the arrogance of the propertied classes. As *The Dark Tunnel* is more openly concerned with evil embodied in the state than is any subsequent book, *Blue City* is more patently distressed by economic tyranny. It marks an incremental step away from a concern for monolithic evil and toward a smaller, more human and personal scale.

The novel offers at least one possible defense against such arrogant economic control in the form of a rare, openly political statement. With the established political system rendered ineffective by the "dreamy idealism" of its mayor, who is incapable of constructive action (a flaw which reappears in a number of Macdonald's characters), meaningful change must be accomplished in other ways, hopefully less vengeful than Weather's. One alternative is suggested by Kaufman, the pawnbroker who has pictures of Marx and Engels on his walls. Kaufman believes that his impromptu lectures on the "exploited masses" can help provide the political and economic education necessary to confront the welter of social ills rampant in the novel. Education in the realities of inequality, Macdonald suggests, is a basis of defense for the dispossessed.

Kaufman also serves to articulate the first real statement in the novels of the ambiguity of evil. Weather is looking for a small-time hood name Joey Sault whom he suspects of being a primary link in the local ring of corruption. Kaufman checks his enthusiasm:

> You simplify too much. . . . Joey is a product of conditions. . . . His father was a cheap bookie, his mother left him young, the gangs in the south side slums brought him up. His sister is a prosperous whore. Naturally he should want to be a pimp. What other use would he have for his good looks?

The caution against oversimplifying and the suggestion that characters are products of conditions (primarily family conditions), and thus only partially responsible for what they have become, expands on the ideas of "giant uncontrollable forces" and "weak men" to include their familial and social origins. Those forces are notably less naturalistic and cosmic than in the previous books. But in *Blue City* there are still signs of external evil drawn in darkest black. For example, Garland, one of the henchmen for the local mob leader, is described as having "looked as if he had been always what he was, as if he had emerged from the womb murderous, cheaply elegant, and epicene." The chief failing of this early book is a lack of subtlety in the portrayal of evil.

In the final scenes, *Blue City*, Weather is proposing marriage and planning to move away from the city he has cleaned up. This conscious decision to move away from the past, having re-assessed it, foreshadows a major aspect of Macdonald's later work and suggests the thesis of the next novel, *The Three Roads*.

*The Three Roads* (1948) is Macdonald's most explicit treatment of his concerns with psychology and the relationships between past, present, and future. Those three stages of time, in fact, constitute one interpretation of the "three roads." The novel also marks the author's most extensive reliance on mythology for plot. The title is taken from Sophocles' classic, *Oedipus Tyrannus*, and the book closely interweaves both the Sophoclean and Freudian versions of the Oedipal story. Since the Oedipus legend plays a role in many of Macdonald's subsequent works, it is helpful to recall it here where the author's use of the myth is most obvious.

Sophocles' story of Oedipus, of course, involves the attempt by Oedipus the King to rid his city, Thebes, of a plague. A soothsayer explains that the plague is being imposed by the gods as retribution for the murder of the former king, Laius. The curse will not be lifted until the murderer is found and punished.

When Laius was king, it had been predicted by an oracle that he would die at the hands of his son. To avert the prophecy, Laius had the child's feet bound and left him on a mountain to die. Many years later, Laius was killed, reportedly by a band of robbers, at the intersection of three roads.

Thebes then fell under the curse of the Sphinx, a frightful half-woman, half-lion, winged monster who confronted travelers with a riddle and devoured them if they could not solve it. The riddle was finally solved by a stranger, Oedipus. The Sphinx died and Oedipus was named king by a grateful people. He married the former king's widow, Jocasta.

Determined to root out the moral blight that has caused the present plague, Oedipus slowly fits together the pieces of the past. He himself had left what he regarded as his native country because he had been told by an oracle that he was destined to kill his father and marry his mother. To escape that prophecy, he left the land where he grew up and the people he knew as his parents. But Oedipus learns that he is, in fact, the abandoned child of Laius and Jocasta. It was he who had confronted Laius at the three roads and unwittingly slain him when their conflicting hubris erupted into battle.

Oedipus has thus, in compliance with the prophecy, killed his father and married his mother. The efforts by both men to avoid their predicted doom only served to fulfill it.

Freud adopted this myth to explain one of the stages of sexual development which he hypothesized in human beings. According to Freud, a male child initially loves his mother and identifies with his father. As sexual urges are heightened, the boy desires the mother incestuously and becomes jealous of the father, his rival. This state of desiring exclusive sexual possession of the mother and feeling antagonistic toward the father is termed the *Oedipus complex*. According to Freud, these feelings are normally repressed about the age of five, because the child comes to fear physical harm (castration in Freud's system) from the father if the desire persists.

Macdonald's fascination with the two aspects of this tale is quite revealing. Sophocles' version emphasizes the overpowering role of fate in the world; Freud's extends that fate to the landscape of the individual psyche. Each individual comes to consciousness within a psychological and mythological fabric. Defining the texture of that fabric is one of Macdonald's primary concerns.

Bret Taylor literally "comes to consciousness" in this novel. He is a veteran of the war in the Pacific who has been hospitalized with amnesia for nine months. Over the course of the novel we observe him, like Oedipus, slowly reassembling the past to arrive at an intersection in time that was so horrible that his mind refuses to recall it.

The device of amnesia permits numerous comments on the past and its proper relation to the present. Taylor's friend Paula says impulsively, at one point: "Forget the past." To which he responds, "I have to remember it first." Macdonald consistently argues for a movement away from the past, but it is an argument for revaluation rather than abandonment. Past and present are inseparable. As one of the doctors in the book remarks, "Past and present are so intertwined that you can't abandon one without losing your grip on the other. Loss of the present is a fair description of insanity. " Loss of the present is also a fair description of the state of mind of many of Macdonald's characters. And it is a striving to restore them to the present via an understanding of the past that informs most of Macdonald's later, finer plots.

To understand Bret Taylor's amnesia, his alienation from the past, requires an understanding of several key events in his life and an appreciation of the family atmosphere in which he grew up. Taylor's background is Midwestern. His father was a shy, secretive, monkish man who gave up religious studies to become a philosophy professor. As Taylor remembers it, his mother died when he was four, leaving him totally dominated by his father and his father's obsession with sexual morality. His father warned him about women, telling him that "there was no virtue in any of them" and that he should "regard them as whited sepulchers, lovely receptacles of the world's filth." The father's state of mind is finally explained by the revelation that Bret's mother did not die. Rather, Bret stumbled into his mother's room after a nightmare and found her in bed with the star boarder. The child "carried on something terrible," beating his mother with his fists, and raised such a disturbance that the father was aroused and found the lovers out. A fight ensued and the mother and boarder ran away together that night. The next day, Bret's father told him that his mother had died.

"Death is a mystery to child's mind, an awesome mystery," Dr. Klifter explains:

> To us, too, it is a mystery, an inexplainable accident, but to a child: May he not have imagined deep in his heart that he had killed his mother with his feeble fists? Such a secret, too dreadful to be spoken of to his stern father, may explain the genesis of his guilt.

The plot forces us to distinguish between types of guilt. Later novels will develop more fully a concept of universal guilt dependent upon such sources as Dostoevsky and the Bible. But there is also a kind of secondary or futile guilt, frequently foisted onto a younger generation at a very impressionable age by their elders. In Macdonald's books this often results in a later crime by the younger in a distorted effort to rationalize the guilt or in order to merit punishment. This later crime characteristically resembles and reflects the earlier crime and echoes the guilt of humanity across generations. As Macdonald has said, "Like the repeated exile of Oedipus, the crucial events of my novel seem to happen at least twice ... setting the whole story in circular motion." Though the comment was made about *The Galton Case*, it applies equally well to *The Three Roads* and, indeed, to most of Macdonald's plots. For Bret Taylor, finding his wife with another man parallels finding his mother with another man. The scene reinforces his father's prejudices against women, and the guilt that he has repressed for his mother's "death" flares up into violent action.

In the final universalizing image, we read of Bret:

He was no more than a tiny mote of darkness in the sun, a
little seed of flesh thrown down between the earth and sky,
blown here and there by the wind of time that swept away the
insect generations of men. He had betrayed his own side in
the unequal war against death, and deserved nothing of anyone. Yet he drew a bitter strength from his humility. He could
say the word 'murderer' to himself and answer to the name.
He could see it was not justice but mercy that he needed.

Though the heavy hand of naturalism is still obvious, the
important realization is of a personal connection with guilt.
Ultimately, in humility there is strength. Mercy is a higher
value than justice. These are integral parts of the Macdonald creed. And in the end, mercy is served. Bret Taylor, like
Oedipus, has found that the man he was looking for is himself. But, mercifully, only the doctors and Paula know the
truth and strict *justice* (in the manner of Sophocles) is not
demanded. As the book ends, Bret says to Paula simply,
"You're very good" and Paula has realized that:

> Things would never be as good as they might once have been,
> but they would be good enough. She had learned not to make
> too great demands on life.

The lessons of this novel are manifold. Violence is often
rooted in guilt. Guilt is often a result of some aberrant
notion of sexuality reinforced at a susceptible age. "Every
man has within him . . . the total range of good and evil. We
all must learn to live with the dreadful fact of our own
selfishness. There is no virtue in futile guilt."

The ending is one of Macdonald's most positive—a man
and woman in love, fully aware of the collective past and
their own individual pasts and limitations, walk arm in arm
up the stairs to bed.

*The Moving Target* (1949) marks several firsts for Macdonald and refines numerous themes which continue to be developed in later novels. It is the first novel in which we find
Lew Archer and the first in which post-war California becomes a critical element of the plot.

Several subsequent novels open in roughly parallel fashion. Archer, a man of very moderate means and of lower-middle class background, is crossing into the land of the wealthy, calling on a client. The place is Cabrillo Canyon. The houses are so distantly scattered and concealed by the landscape that Archer asks of his cab driver if "the people live in caves." A sign on the road advises: "Private Property: Permission to pass over revocable at any time." The power of money and the arrogance of the modern ego conspire in this world to create the illusion of human dominance over nature, but the ultimate effect is of a world outside reality. Archer says:

> A Rolls with a doll at the wheel went by us like a gust of wind, and I felt unreal.
> The light-blue haze in the lower canyon was like a thin smoke from slowly burning money.... Private property: color guaranteed fast: will not shrink egos. I had never seen the Pacific look so small.

By contrast, when he leaves this promontory of the wealthy, Archer finds himself driving

> through a mile of slums: collapsing shacks and storefront tabernacles, dirt paths where sidewalks should have been, black and brown children playing in the dust.... After Cabrillo Canyon I felt like a man from another planet.

A consciousness of the ostracizing powers of money is never far from Macdonald's plots.

*The Moving Target* marks a sharp turn of those plots toward greater complexity. In the novel immediately preceding, *The Three Roads*, there is one central murder and one basic story line. In *The Moving Target*, plot lines and murders multiply.

The figure who attracts central attention in the early part of the novel is an older man named Sampson. He is bored with his life and his wealth derived from Oklahoma and Texas oil wells and seeks meaning or "kicks" via an extramarital sexual liaison set in a private bungalow decorated in an astrological motif with red drapes and furniture, red lights, and a ceiling mirror. Archer says of the room that "it made me angry." He describes it as looking "like the inside of a sick brain, with no eyes to see out of, nothing to look at but the upside-down reflection of itself." This "sick brain" objectified in the room provides a crystalline, imagistic device for exploring the personal corruption at the heart of a foundering society. Sampson has the means at his disposal to accomplish great things. But his drive is all inward, and his money has only allowed him to cut himself off from external responsibility. His selfishness runs to such extremes that he is left with a distorted, upside-down reflection of his ego within which to live out his fantasy. We never actually see Sampson in the book until he is dead. But his selfish life and activities permeate the plot.

One element of this multifaceted plot concerns the smuggling of Mexicans across the border as tenant farmers and strikebreakers. The irony is that Sampson's father had been a tenant farmer; Sampson himself had started with nothing, and now that he's a wealthy man "he can't seem to see that Mexican field-workers are people." Running parallel to the people-smuggling plot is one of kidnapping. And complicating the entire story is a love triangle between Sampson's daughter Miranda, his attorney Bert Graves, and Alan Taggert, his pilot and substitute son. Sampson's real son was a pilot killed in the war.

The effect of the war on the men who fought it and utimately on the society they came home to inhabit gets further attention here. The lawyer Graves homes in on the subject in a passage in which he is describing Taggert. He says he has "seen this same thing happen to other boys," and explains:

> War was their element, and when the war was finished, they were finished. They had to go back to boys' jobs and take orders from middle-aged civilians. . . . Some of them couldn't take it and went bad. . . . They wanted to be free and happy and successful without laying any foundation for freedom or happiness or success. And there's the hangover.

In addition to the war as a root cause of the modern condition, there is money. "Money is the lifeblood in this town.
If you don't have it you're only half alive." And beyond
money, there is something else. "You can't blame money for
what it does to people. The evil is in people, and money is
the peg they hang it on. They go wild for money when
they've lost their other values." But even this internal evil

> isn't so simple. Everybody has it in him, and whether it comes
> out in his actions depends on a number of things. Environ-
> ment, opportunity, economic pressure, a piece of bad luck, a
> wrong friend.

*The Moving Target* is a major step in Macdonald's portrayal of the complexities and ambiguities of evil. In this
novel there is no one crime. And though the plot does finally
uncover one character whose greed is responsible for the
several deaths in the book, there is no one villain; the motivations of evil are diversified and diffuse.

*The Drowning Pool* (1950) draws together two distinct
themes that gradually come to dominate Macdonald's writings. One is an extension of individual greed to corporate
greed and technological rape of the landscape. In *The Drowning Pool,* this concern is defined by the oil magnate Kilbourne who used the war era to make his fortune in black
market cars in Detroit and then fled to California to protect
his wealth by investing it legitimately. "Now he's grand old
California stock and politicians go to his parties." He is also
presently involved in the oil business and responsible for
the construction of "the latticed triangles of the derricks
where trees had grown, the oil pumps nodding and clanking
where cattle had grazed."
   The other dominant motif involves an adolescent, Cathy
Slocum, caught in the middle of a hopelessly neurotic domestic situation. The principal members of this family are
a grandmother, mother, father, and Cathy. The grandmother is a tight-fisted, tyrannical matriarch who doles out
just enough money to her son to keep him on a string. The

mother is caught between a desire for the storybook love affair (with another woman's husband) and the harsh reality of life with her self-centered spouse. The father is a rather simple-minded man with dilettantish ideas about acting, an implied homosexual leaning, and no greater goal than waiting for his mother to die and the estate to be probated.

The family plot is resolved by a device related to the Oedipal myth—the mistaken father. *The Drowning Pool* marks Macdonald's first use of this device which will reappear and which finds its most extensive elaboration in the pivotal novel, *The Galton Case.* The technological aspect of the plot is resolved through a flaw in the system's technical devices. An unforeseen structural weakness in the water therapy room in which Archer is to be drowned thwarts the plan and sets up Kilbourne to be shot. Dramatically, if not too obviously, the family is restored and technology defeats itself.

But the book is also largely concerned with the interrelationships between people. Its final scene offers a glimpse into the male psyche that controls the world. Knudson, the police chief, feels compelled to engage in a physical battle with Archer to release his pent-up anger. "It was a long hard fight, and a useless one. Still it had to be fought through." When the fight is over and both men are lying exhausted and congratulating each other on their physical abilities, Archer says: "Around us and above us the darkness was immense. Our hands groped for each other and met. I left him there." It is a part of the masculine mystique, grown out of war and ages of cultural conditioning, that men resolve their problems and effect a catharsis of their frustrations through physical violence. Archer would prefer to avoid the scene ("Bloodletting won't help either of us"), but is at the same time drawn to it ("If you insist"). In the end, there is the faintest note of a new camaraderie and the possibility of human understanding in the last touching of the hands. But there is also the vast darkness. Establishing communication between human beings is a fragile undertaking. While the touching of hands suggests a desire for, perhaps the possibility of, establishing such communication, the "immense darkness" suggests that physical violence is not the path to rapport. Though Archer finds himself drawn to the masculine trap, he is able, finally, to walk away from it.

*The Drowning Pool* also offers Macdonald the opportunity to comment on the creative elements of our society. James Slocum, Cathy's "father," is in rehearsal for a new play called *The Ironist* in which he plays the lead and which mocks the real life of the novel in a cheap and corny fashion. It was "the kind of stuff that parodied itself. Phony sophistication with a high gloss, and no insides at all." In the party scene following the play, we find the best paragraph Macdonald has yet written on the subject of the intellectual atrophy of the idle classes. Archer is standing back out of the flow.

> I listened to them talk. Existentialism, they said. Henry Miller and Truman Capote and Henry Moore. Andre Gide and Anais Nin and Djuna Barnes. And sex—hard-boiled, poached, coddled, shirred, and fried easy over in sweet, fresh creamery butter. Sex solo, in duet, trio, quartet; for all-male chorus; for choir and symphony; and played on the harpsichord in three-fourths time. And Albert Schweitzer and the dignity of everything that lives.

Sex, philosophy, literature, music, art are all swiftly juxtaposed and reduced to the absurdity of tinkling cocktail conversation. Money has made possible the "artistic freedom" which these characters enjoy. That freedom appears inevitably converted to a de-humanized, de-personalized obsession with sex. All values are diminished to a peripheral position in relation to the two great forces—"sex and money: the forked root of evil."

*The Way Some People Die* (1951) shifts away from the author's concern for the wealthy in society to a portrayal of organized criminal elements—from those who handle heroin in large quantities to those who operate the local pinball and wrestling rackets.

In the wrestling motif Macdonald finds a forum for commenting on the consciousness of a much lower stratum of society than the would-be actors, writers, and critics who attracted his barbed analysis in *The Drowning Pool*. Archer arrives at the arena to find a great crowd witnessing "the weekly battle between right and wrong." As the match draws to a close:

> Redbeard, felled by the breeze or the idea of the kick, went down heavily on his back. Right landed neatly on the back of its neck and sprang to its feet in triumph like a tumbler. Wrong lay prostrate while the referee counted it out and declared Right the winner. The crowd cheered.

This stylized battle scene offers much the same critique of the mass mind as does war. People seem to prefer, if not demand, a simplistic explanation of good and evil, of right and wrong. They are seeing what they want to see. What they fail to perceive, of course, is that they are being exploited by an organized criminal element for the purpose of making a profit. The scene suggests that economic status is not the sole determinant of political oppression of the masses. Such oppression is endemic. So long as people prefer the illusion of simplicity to the reality of complexity, they are subject to exploitation by whatever powers or groups comprehend this weakness.

This novel also expands on the theme of male-female conflicts, another central concern of the later novels. Galatea (Galley) Lawrence is a central figure. Near the end of the novel, she has reason to hold a gun on Archer and he comments:

> a single gun in the hands of a woman like Galley was the most dangerous weapon. Only the female sex was human in her eyes, and she was its only important member.

To comprehend the impact of this statement, it is helpful to recall an earlier scene in which Dowser, the macho crime boss, is playing cards with one of his girlfriends, Irene, and cheating. When she complains, he threatens her. When she apologizes and attempts to continue the game, he becomes indignant and explodes, "Why should I play you for it when I can take it any time I want?" Such tirades are the essence of the irrational brutalization of women by men throughout recorded history.

We are never really given sufficient background information to understand Galley and her threatening actions, to understand why "only the female sex was human in her eyes." Certainly we are not given the extensive psychological background that later novels will provide for such significant characters. But for readers who demand explanations for actions, the clue is there and fairly obvious. It is in the name Galatea. In an ancient tale told by Ovid, Galatea is the creation of a young Cypriot sculptor, Pygmalion, who hates women. But he devotes his life and genius to the creation of a perfect woman in stone. He is successful beyond his wildest dreams. He falls in love with his creation and strives to bring her to life, but she remains hopelessly cold and lifeless.

It might be argued that women are often products of a male idea rooted in illusion and misogyny. Men like Dowser certainly tend to perpetuate the travesty. And it can hardly be surprising that living women, like Galley, can be cold and unsympathetic in life and persuaded that the female sex is the only human one.

There are many attempts in this book to explore the social fiber and interpret its meaning. The interpretation of the mass consciousness through the wrestling scenes and the elucidation of the archetypal male-female conflict through Galley and Dowser are only two of those. Another comes by way of Archer's musings on Dowser himself, as he tries to fathom the source of his power and the reason for his longevity. He finds it curious that such men can acquire and maintain such authority:

No doubt they got the power because they wanted it so badly, and were willing to . . . run any risk, for the sake of seizing power and holding on. They would bribe public officials, kill off rivals, peddle women and drugs; and they were somehow

tolerated because they did these things for money and success,
not for the things themselves.

Such men are tolerated because they operate from a stance
which embodies the American Dream. They do what they
do for money and success, and the popular reaction is not to
overthrow them but to stand in awe and envious admiration
of the principles of aggrandizement so well executed.

By the end of *The Way Some People Die*, the plot has come
around again to Mrs. Lawrence's sitting room where it
began. There "above the date-palms, half-hidden in space,"
an "unknown bird" is describing "its dark circles." Macdonald's highly structured plots often describe circles, and
every one has its dark side.

*The Ivory Grin* (1952) is remarkable for its foreshadowing
of a basic element of *The Galton Case* (the idealistic son in
revolt against guilt and his wealthy parents) and for its
treatment of blacks.

Charles Singleton, Jr., the son of very wealthy parents,
served as a pilot in the war. His father is dead. Since his
return from the conflict he has embarked on the mission of
separating himself from his mother and creating a life of
his own. We are told that he feels guilty about having so
much money which he never worked for and that he

> had different ideas from his father. He believed that he and
> his class were out of touch with reality. That they had to save
> their individual souls by going down to the bottom of things
> and starting all over.

He began his descent to the bottom of things by taking a
job as a tomato picker. That experiment ended in a fight
with the foreman and Charles's coming home with his face
bashed. The war theme is re-enforced in the remarks of
Sylvia, the house girl: "For a man who shot down enemy
planes during the war, he's such a child, such a dreamer."
Archer repeats this assessment in his reflections on Singleton near the end of the novel: "It's possible he was out of

touch with his own standards . . . he sounds flawed to me—
a man trying all his life to get hold of something real and
not succeeding." Idealism is the tragic flaw in many of Macdonald's characters of the war generation. It would appear
that the war itself impressed them with the possibility of
moral action on a grand scale. But back in the everyday
world they find that on an individual level their ideals far
outstrip their real power to affect the state of the world. A
war machine and a war mentality tend to oversimplify the
world much in the fashion of the crowds at the wrestling
match in *The Way Some People Die.* In war there are win-
ners and losers, right and wrong; in life, Macdonald says
more and more eloquently as the novels progress, everything is gray. To have black-and-white goals can only lead
to frustration and self-destruction. The tragic flaw in any
character is not to recognize reality for what it is—complex,
rooted in the vagaries of human nature, slow to change,
imperfectable.

This novel also marks the first major attempt by Macdonald to portray persons from outside the dominant white
male culture, and thereby to comment on that culture. In
an early scene, Archer is wandering through a black neighborhood in search of leads. He tells people that he is making
a survey of radio listeners. One older black woman invites
him to "Come in and sit down. I like to make new friends,"
and then regales him with tales of her "twelve grandchil-
dren, six great-grandchildren, more on the way." All this is
in marked contrast to Macdonald's white characters who, in
book after book, insist "I have no friends" and whose families are fragmented and at war, totally unlike the continuity of generations which the black woman describes.

Later in the novel, when Alex Norris, a young black male,
is suspected of murdering Lucy Champion (his girlfriend),
the local police chief has him handcuffed to her body in the
morgue and leaves him there to await a confession. Alex's
reaction is a quiet, strong passivity. The police lieutenant
is querulous because "the boy by accepting everything had
turned the tables on him." Archer comments about Alex
that his expression was "beyond the reach of anything

white men could do or say. He nodded wordlessly, and looked back at Lucy."

It is a commonplace that the dominant force in our society is white and male. Blacks have centuries of experience with being enslaved and oppressed at the hands of that force. We see in *The Ivory Grin* the suggestion that such people make a powerful and moving comment on our culture. They have learned the power of acceptance and passivity, and they have a deeper awareness of the complexity and imperfectability of reality than newborn idealists like Charles Singleton. That awareness sustains them while the Charles Singletons of the world frequently find themselves doomed to an untimely death.

*Meet Me at the Morgue* (1953) involves Macdonald's second treatment of the misplaced father story and does so without the use of Archer as protagonist. It is the first of two occasions after the creation of Archer (*The Ferguson Affair* is the other) in which Macdonald chose to use another central figure.

The story involves Macdonald's tightest plotting to this point and returns briefly to the device of the chase scene in one of the fastest-paced vignettes he has yet written. It is another story which finds its roots in the war.

The exclusion of Archer is certainly one of the most intriguing aspects of this novel in that his absence allows Macdonald to comment on his famous detective at a distance. The protagonist in this book is Howie Cross, a probation officer. At one point, an FBI man, Forest, warns Cross about private detectives: "You never can tell about these private operators. The dirt they work in is always rubbing off on them." Though, in this case, he is talking about a man named Bourke and is right, we can hardly help feel that Archer is being talked about behind his back.

But in a more significant passage, Cross is trying to respond to Helen Johnson's question: "What sort of man are you, Mr. Cross?" Initially he says, "I'm a slightly displaced person, I think. Nothing quite suits me, or rather I don't quite suit." As he has a moment longer to think about the question, he reflects that his parents had a bad marriage and that that is somehow responsible for his feeling "more strongly for other people than I do for myself." As his reflections continue, he is recalling his college career in sociology:

> I wanted to help people. Helpfulness was like a religion with a lot of us in those days. It's only in the last few years, since the war, that I've started to see around it. I see that helping other people can be an evasion of oneself, and the source of a good deal of smug self-satisfaction. But it takes the emotions a long time to catch up. I'm emotionally rather backward.

Such self-consciousness is of a higher order than anything yet articulated by Archer. It marks, on the part of the author, a new level of reflection on the motivations of his intermediary. Macdonald's purpose, on its grandest scale, might be described as an effort to depict the relationships between the psychological framework of the individual and the sociological framework of society. Such an endeavor would be doomed to failure without some recognition of the psychological idiosyncrasies, the humanity, of his narrator. Archer himself progressively develops the refined self-consciousness necessary to such a task, but Howie Cross represents a distinct stage in that development.

Archer's exclusion serves another purpose, which becomes apparent at the novel's end. Cross, much like Archer, has his difficulties relating meaningfully to women in the book. In the early chapters he has a romantic interest, but she proves to be interested in another man. By the end of the book, he has developed a new romantic relationship and is contemplating marriage. As the two of them drive back toward the city, he muses, "Her body lay away from me in the seat like a mysterious country I had dreamed of all my life." There is definite hope that some union may be forged between this "dreamer" and the "mysterious country." But it is the kind of ending which Macdonald will not attempt with Archer until *The Blue Hammer*—and there only tentatively. The problem underscores an inherent limitation of the recurring narrator. Allowing Archer to marry could well involve complications for future novels. Thus it is Cross who must march toward matrimony rather than Archer.

*Find a Victim* (1954) marks the return of Archer in one of Macdonald's most striking opening images and one of his most rapidly developing plots. As Archer is driving through Las Cruces on his way to Sacramento, he passes a man dying on the side of the road: "He was the ghastliest hitchhiker who ever thumbed me." Immediately the plot becomes immersed in the implications of smuggling and love triangles. But the primary concern of the plot is elaborating the epigraph from Stephen Crane:

> A man feared that he might find an assassin;
> Another that he might find a victim.
> One was more wise than the other.

The implication is that the wiser man sees beyond the mere fact of assassination to the root causes of the killing; the assassin *is* the victim.

And in this case the assassin is a woman whose violent actions are manifestations of the psychological violence done to her by men. Macdonald offers us some capsule comments on the nature of this violence. In describing the father figure in the book, he says:

> His living room was the kind of room you find in back-country ranch-houses where old men hold the last frontier against women and civilization and hygiene.... The double-barreled shotgun over the mantel was the only clean and cared-for object in the room.

At another point, a female character remarks:

> Most of the men in this city are barbarians where women are concerned. It's a wretched place for a girl to try and grow up. It's like living among savages.

The novel readily supports such assertions: one central female figure was assaulted by her father when she was fifteen, was moved by the court authorities to live with her sister and brother-in-law, and then grew up to be the mistress of that brother-in-law.

The "masculine" plot which counter-balances the sexual intrigue and feminine oppression of the novel concerns the stealing of a truckload of whiskey with the ultimate goal of selling it to the Indians on the reservation. Since the Indians won't be concerned with the illegality of the transaction, a quick, easy profit can be had.

The entirety of the smuggling plot has a simplistic "cowboys and Indians" quality about it and ends with a ghost town shoot-out reminiscent of stereotypical Western movies. Men play games; their women go crazy. And there can be little surprise that one of the women's frustrations ultimately erupts into violence.

*The Barbarous Coast* (1956) takes on the decadence of Hollywood as subject and continues to broaden the social range and deepen the moral complexity of Macdonald's vision.

There is considerable social history behind the principal characters of the book. The movie producer is a Greek whose name has been shortened to Graff, very close to "graft." The manager of the Channel Club, where much of the action takes place, is Clarence Bassett, a man who has been writing a family history. His ancestors landed in Massachusetts in 1634. But these descendants of such noble lines only spawn depravity and violence in contemporary California. A writer who works for Graff's studio laments at a party:

"*Salammbo* is a tragedy, its theme is dissolution. So Sime Graff tells me to tack a happy ending onto it. And I write it that way. Jesus. . . . What makes me do it to myself and Flaubert? I used to worship Flaubert."
"Money?" I said.
"Yeah. Money. Money." He repeated the word several times, with varying inflections. He seemed to be finding new shades of meaning in it, subtle drunken personal meanings which brought the tears into his voice.

Even the Greeks, founders of Western art, are now corruptors of that art and contributors to barbarism. And a descendant of the colonists, Charles Bassett, is now so involved in illicit sexual affairs that the ultimate outcome is death.

On the grandest scale, *The Barbarous Coast* strives to comment on the total sweep of history toward a seemingly inevitable decline. And though the novel makes its strongest statement in terms of the personal lives and predicaments of individual characters, that sense of historical connectedness and a certain perversion of the positive possibilities of the past are over-riding themes in the Macdonald canon.

It is interesting to note, from a biographical perspective, the conjunction of certain elements of this book and Macdonald's own life. In his preface to *Archer in Hollywood* (1967), an omnibus reprint of *The Moving Target*, *The Way Some People Die*, and *The Barbarous Coast*, Macdonald says:

> *The Barbarous Coast* was written when I was forty.... In it I was learning to get rid of the protective wall between my mind and the perilous stuff of my own life.
>
> I'm not and never was George Wall, the angry young Canadian lost in Hollywood. But I once lived, as George did, on Spadina Avenue in Toronto. Like the three young divers in the story, I was a tower diver before my bones got brittle. And I once went to a party not wholly unlike the long party in the book.

In all these "early novels," the perceptive reader may note the "protective wall" between the author and what will become his primary material in later novels—the family. These earlier works tend to take an isolated autobiographical fact—like being a diver, being in the Navy, traveling in Germany—and use it as the foundation for an experiment along various tangents of the detective form. *The Dark Tunnel*, for example, concerns itself with the state as evil; *Blue City* tackles the subjects of class distinction and political corruption; *The Three Roads* explores individual psychology and guilt, and so on. Macdonald has noted the difficulty he experienced in trying to write a purely autobiographical statement and credited the creation of Archer with freeing him from that psychic bind. After writing eleven novels, reaching the age of forty, experiencing a time of psychological trauma, and finding therapeutic release in a period of psychoanalysis, he begins to be able to use the shield of Archer to explore evil within the more personal context of the family. All the themes of the early novels—alienation, the past, male-female relationships, political and economic tyranny—coalesce within this basic frame. Because the family is the essential context of human experience, the subject matter becomes more universal. By confronting the unusual patterns of his own life and family, Macdonald achieves a sympathetic awareness which allows him to construct family plots which are at once bizarre and believable. Locating evil within the individual and in the family structure out of which he or she developed defines the cohesion of Macdonald's later works, provides a base for his mythologizing tendencies, and marks his development from a lesser to a greater artist. The first eleven novels bear all the marks of the artist who created the later works, but they lack the centrality of purpose which becomes evident only in those later novels. The early works are fragments of a world view which achieves unity only after the author himself achieves unity with his own past.

# Public Evil and Private Terrors

## *The Galton Case* and Other Major Novels

> It's a complex world. The human mind is
> the most complex thing in it.
> *The Chill*

Macdonald considers *The Galton Case* to have marked his
transition from the conventional detective form to his own
interpretation of that tradition and his own fictional system. *The Doomsters* is clearly a foreshadowing of that break.
Through these next seven novels, the author's world view is
molded into a unified vision of human crime, guilt, and suffering rooted in individual psychology and the family and
spilling over into the fledgling society of California. *The
Zebra-Striped Hearse* and *The Chill* are sterling achievements of this period.

*The Doomsters* (1958) is Macdonald's first extensive explo-
ration of the family saga as plot. Elements of this concern
for family appeared as early as *The Drowning Pool*, but it
is in *The Doomsters* that the concept takes on the full range
of complexity toward which Macdonald's work tends.

The novel deals with the Hallman family of the California
town of Purissima ("most pure"). Carl Hallman is the idealistic son. His father sent him initially to the University of
California at Davis to study agriculture in order to be able
to run the family ranch; he flunked out there and then made
his way to Berkeley to study philosophy. His period at
Berkeley is three years in the past when the novel opens.
While at Berkeley, he disappeared mysteriously for about
ten days just about the time his mother died under somewhat unusual circumstances. In the spring before the novel

40

opens, his father was killed, and Carl has been institution-
alized in the state hospital ever since as the murder suspect. The hospital setting recalls *The Three Roads* and its
Oedipal theme, which will receive extensive development in
this novel.

In the opening scenes, Archer's psychic state is placed
squarely within the society's neurotic norm. He is dreaming
of "a hairless ape who lived in a cage by himself," kept in
"a state of nervous tension" by the people who are "always
trying to get in." Carl Hallman is knocking on his door. He
has just broken out of the hospital and has sought out
Archer on the advice of Tom Rica, a mutual acquaintance.

Carl is obviously not quite stable enough to function in
the real world. He is easily angered and appears to confuse
Archer with his father. He is uncertain about what he wants
Archer to do for him although he finally suggests hiring
him to find out who really killed his father. Archer persuades him to go back to the hospital as a condition for
taking the case.

On the road to the hospital, Carl explains his political
discord with his father, a "frugal Pennsylvania German"
who came west after the First World War, bought a small
orange grove, married into a family with far more land, and
eventually became a local political boss and state senator.
On the night of his father's death, they argued over his
"lousy labor policy" which included shuttling whole families
of migrant Mexican farm workers around in open trucks
like cattle. Carl says his father "never thought in terms of
the human cost" and further elaborates the political theme:

> ... I'm ashamed to say it, but my father cheated some of his
> own best friends, Japanese people. ... They were driven out
> during the war, and never came back. Father bought up their
> land at a few cents on the dollar.
>
> I told him when I got my share of the ranch, I'd give those
> people their property back. ... It doesn't *belong* to us. ...
> We've got to set things right, between us and the land, be-
> tween us and the other people.

Before they reach the hospital, Carl panics, forcibly takes

Archer's car and leaves him unconscious in a ditch. After a visit to the hospital and another to Carl's wife, Mildred, Archer shortly finds himself at the Hallman ranch where Carl has reportedly been spotted wielding a gun. At the ranch, all the major characters come together for the first time. Carl's wife Mildred; Jerry Hallman, Carl's brother; Jerry's wife, Zinnie; the family doctor, Dr. Grantland; and the local sheriff, Ostervelt, are all present. The family shows every evidence of coming apart. Grantland and Zinnie appear to be carrying on a love affair. Jerry threatens Grantland with a pair of garden shears. At one point, Carl is seen running through the grove adjacent to the house with a gun, and, shortly after, Jerry is shot in the greenhouse. There are no witnesses.

As facts are pieced together, suspicion shifts heavily to Dr. Grantland, whose motivations appear to fit the typical mold of evil in Macdonald's world—sex (with Jerry's wife, Zinnie) and money (from the settling of the Hallman estate). Grantland also appears to be involved in drug trafficking.

In a conversation with Miss Parish, Carl's therapist at the state hospital, Archer is convinced that Carl could not possibly have killed either his father or his mother, although he does suffer crippling guilt complexes associated with both deaths. The explanation is Oedipal. Carl wanted to punish himself for his father-killing fantasies. He blames himself for upsetting his father in their argument and thus contributing to his death. And his absence during his mother's death provoked similar guilt in relation to that event.

But Carl is the object of a manhunt nonetheless. In the course of it, another body, Zinnie's, shows up. A hunch takes Archer first to Dr. Grantland's office and then to Grantland's house, where he catches him cleaning up the blood from Zinnie's murder. Grantland claims he didn't do it, but in the course of the scene he knocks Archer unconscious, sets the house afire, and leaves. Archer manages to escape the fire and catches up with Grantland at Mildred's, where Carl is discovered to have been hiding out since Jerry's murder. Just as Archer drives up, Grantland shoots Carl,

wounding him seriously, and is himself shot and killed by
the sheriff.

In the aftermath, Archer learns from a talk with Mildred's
mother that Mildred had lost a baby about three years before, roughly the time of Mrs. Hallman's death. Dr. Grantland was the attending physician; "he treated her real nice,
never even sent her a bill." Archer begins to have one of
his shocking recognitions where he sees the pieces of the
puzzle and mangled lives come clashing together in fearful
clarity:

> A pit or tunnel had opened in my mind, three years deep or
> long. Under white light at the bottom of it, fresh and vivid as
> a hallucination, I could see the red spillage where life had died
> and murder had been born.

He approaches Mildred. "Go away and leave me alone,"
she says. "A lot of people have. Maybe that's the trouble,"
Archer replies. Under the pressure of the day's events and
the influence of Archer's genuine interest in her, Mildred
breaks down and tells everything. She is the killer.

She explains that she gave herself to Carl initially because he was afraid of going homosexual and needed her.
She also confesses to a fascination with his family's wealth.
When Carl went away to Berkeley, she followed him and
finally managed to get pregnant, thinking that would solve
all their problems.

When she told Carl about her pregnancy, "he was afraid
of what his mother would do" and ran away. When Carl
didn't come back, she called his mother and told her of her
pregnancy and that they would have to get married. The
mother was initially irate and hung up. But she called back
in a curiously apologetic mood and suggested that they meet
and discuss the situation. At the meeting, she sympathized
with Mildred's problem and suggested that there was no
reason to "go to all the trouble of having a child if he was
going to live in grief, cut off from the stars. Or if his daddy
was never coming back." Mildred found herself entranced
by the mother's hypnotic voice and went along to Dr. Grant-

land's office even though she began to comprehend that abortion was Mrs. Hallman's intention. When she was already on the table and realized it was too late, she made an effort to stop it.

> I screamed and fought against him. She came into the room with that gun of hers and told me to lie down and be quiet, or she'd kill me on the spot. Dr. Grantland didn't want to go through with it. She said if he didn't she'd run him out of his practice. He put a needle in me.

When Mildred came out of the anesthesia, she picked up a bottle in her half-drugged state, and smashed the mother over the head with it. She assumes she killed her. Grantland told her later that he had thrown the body in the sea to make it look like suicide and said that "it would set the seal on our friendship if we went to bed together."

Shortly after, Mildred and Carl moved back to Oakland and got married. But Carl lapsed into another black depression and finally moved back home. She followed him and lived in the Hallman house for two years. But Grantland had his hold over her by then and his own designs on the Hallman fortune. He suggested to her that things would work much more smoothly if the Senator were dead. As Mildred remembers it:

> He didn't tell me outright that I had to kill the Senator. I didn't have to be told. I didn't even have to think about it. I simply let myself forget who I was, and went through the whole thing like clockwork.

At least part of her motivation involved a hatred for her own father who had deserted her family when she was a child. Her hatred was easily transferred. She also admits to shooting Jerry, under Grantland's direction, to simplify the settling of the family estate.

Finally Mildred lost faith in Grantland and went to his house intending to kill him. But, "Zinnie happened to be the one who was there. I killed her, I hardly know why. I felt ashamed for her, lying naked like that in his bed. It was almost like killing myself."

Heavy emphasis is given throughout the book to the psychological motivations for action. Behind most of Mildred's deeds are a fatherless childhood, the monetary envy of the dispossessed, and an horrific abortion at gunpoint. And Macdonald spares no effort to give us a psychological portrait of the woman behind the gun, Alicia Hallman. In a conversation with Mrs. Hutchinson, her nurse, we are told that she "was the saddest woman you ever want to see, specially toward the end there. She got the idea in her head that nobody loved her, nobody ever *did* love her." And later, Mrs. Hutchinson recalls:

> She was always talking about those Doomsters of hers. She believed her life was ruled by evil fates like, and they had killed all the love in the world the day that she was born.

Mrs. Hallman is a portrait of a woman who has walled herself off from—or been walled off by—the rest of the world, convinced that she is unloved, that love does not exist. And where love does not exist, there is incredible license to create horrors and death for others, to spread one's own misery.

Macdonald suggests that a lack of love is at the bottom of the horror of *The Doomsters*. And it does not end with Mrs. Hallman. Mildred, at one point, describes her experience in bed with Carl: "The spirit rose up from me and floated over the bed. I looked down and watched Carl using my body. And I hated him. He didn't love *me*. He didn't want to know *me*." In another passage, Archer is driving through town and observes a boy on a ladder changing "the shabby marquee of the Mexican movie house. AMOR was the only word that was left. He started to take that down." Love is the only word left; when that goes there will be nothing. Carl's reaction to a lack of love is the acceptance of a futile guilt for his parents' deaths and an attempt to *use* Mildred's body to *make* love. Jerry, Zinnie, and Grantland react to this lack by channeling their efforts toward the realization of personal wealth, regardless of the human costs. When Mrs. Hallman and Mildred experience the lack of love, murder follows.

The frightening thing is that the guilt, the inhumanity, the lack of love, the violence which are manifested in the Hallman family are passed from generation to generation. The story actually begins with the father's movement westward, forgetting his own humble beginnings and humanity in the process. His aspirations turned to money and power and were not tempered by a concern for the human beings whose exploitation was necessary to achieve his ends. He even married for money and contributed to the psychic destruction of his wife by using her rather than loving her. In the next generation, the conflict between his idealist offspring, Carl, and Jerry, whose greed matches his own, erupts in death and destruction. Mrs. Hutchinson sees this chain as the fulfillment of a prophecy and quotes the Biblical axiom, "The fathers have eaten sour grapes, and the children's teeth are set on edge." To which Miss Parish responds "Right out of Freud." And to which we might add, "Pure Macdonald." Increasingly in the novels, this sense of the sins of the fathers being visited upon the children becomes dominant. *The Doomsters* marks Macdonald's boldest effort to this point to portray the complexities of motivation within a family tragedy. The novel draws its own conclusions. Archer is thinking:

> The current of guilt flowed in a closed circuit if you traced it far enough.
>
> Thinking of Alicia Hallman and her open-ended legacy of death, I was almost ready to believe in her doomsters. If they didn't exist in the actual world they rose from the depths of every man's inner sea, gentle as night dreams, with the back-breaking force of tidal waves. Perhaps they existed in the sense that men and women were their own doomsters, the secret authors of their own destruction. You had to be very careful what you dreamed.

The patriarch of the Hallman family dreamed of creating his own autonomous, idyllic world. He dreamed the basic, selfish dream of modern America. He made no allowances for the complexities of relationships between men and women, the propertied and the laborers, or disparate generations. His self-absorption doomed a family.

Macdonald considers *The Doomsters* to have "marked a fairly clean break with the Chandler tradition . . . and freed me to make my own approach to the crimes and sorrows of life." His next novel, his thirteenth, is of such singular importance in the development of his art that he has written an essay entitled "Writing *The Galton Case*."

He begins the essay with an effort to describe the kind of irrational, subconscious motivators which he sees behind human actions in general and his plots in particular. He speaks of a night when he was baby-sitting with his five-year-old grandson, Jimmie. Jimmie was staging a one-man performance, the main idea of which

> seemed to be to express and discharge his guilts and fears, particularly his over-riding fear that his absent parents might punish his *(imperceptible) moral imperfections* by never coming back to him. (Emphasis added)

Jimmie hid behind an armchair and popped out with a towel over his head crying "I'm a monster" and then dissolved into laughter until, "soothed and purged by his simple but powerful art," he fell asleep.

Macdonald believes that we all have a sense of a private monster which we desire to purge, and he draws a parallel between the child's drama and the art of self-disguise that is a central element of serious detective fiction:

> Disguise is the imaginative device which permits the work to be both private and public, to half-divulge the writer's crucial secrets while deepening the whole community's sense of its own mysterious life.

In *The Galton Case* (1959), many of the writer's crucial secrets are half-divulged and a considerable deepening of the mysterious life of the community is achieved through the scrutiny of three generations of the Galton family.

*The Galton Case* begins as the story of a 73-year-old woman of great wealth with little time to live who desires to be reconciled with her son from whom she parted "in bitter anger and hatred" on the eleventh day of October 1936, twenty-three years in the past. The son, Anthony Galton, had been forced to study mechanical engineering but rebelled because "he wanted to go away and write."

In a series of statements early in the novel which reflect great irony, considering what happens subsequently to this idealistic young man, we are told by the housegirl, Cassie Hildreth:

> Tony disapproved of expatriates. He always said he wanted to get *closer* to America. This was in the depression, remember. He was very strong for the rights of the working class. . . .
>
> He did feel that having money cut him off from life. . . . He often said he wanted to live like ordinary people, lose himself in the mass.

And later she says:

> He had a theory that the country was going through another civil war—a war between the rich people and the poor people. He thought of the poor people as white Negroes, and he wanted to do for them what John Brown did for the slaves. Lead them out of bondage—in the spiritual sense, of course. Tony didn't believe in violence.

Archer is employed initially by Gordon Sable, attorney for Mrs. Galton, who is described as a man who "specialized in estate work, and moved in circles where money was seen but not heard." As the story opens, a man is murdered at Sable's house. The victim is Sable's houseman, Peter Culligan. When Archer met Culligan just prior to his murder, he described him as having a "trouble-prone" face which "invited violence, as certain other people invite friendship." At the outset it is not at all clear whether Culligan's death has any bearing on the Galton case. The circumstances are mysterious. Only Sable's wife Alice is said to have been at home at the time. An unknown man in a black Jaguar is said to have driven up, rung the doorbell, stabbed Culligan and driven off. By the time Archer arrives back at the Sable house, Alice is near hysteria.

As Archer pursues the Galton case, he finds himself at Luna Bay just south of San Francisco, Galton's last known address. He had lived there under the assumed name of John Brown with his wife Teddy and infant son until about Christmas 1936, when they disappeared. Teddy was the girl whom Galton/Brown had brought home with him on his last visit and who had been totally unacceptable to his mother. Teddy had also been involved with members of a depression-era gangland group operating out of the Red Horse Inn at Luna Bay who thrived on smuggling during the height of Prohibition.

One of the first things Archer discovers there is that during recent excavation for a new shopping center, a skeleton was turned up near the site of the Brown house. The skeleton is complete except that the skull is missing. The probability exists that the victim was decapitated with an ax.

Through a healed fracture in one of the bones, the body is positively identified as that of Anthony Galton, alias John Brown. In a virtually simultaneous development which stretches even Archer's acceptance of coincidence, a young man shows up who claims to be John Brown, Jr. The boy says that he grew up in an orphanage in Ohio, where he was left by his mother at four. He claims to have run away from there at sixteen and gone to Ann Arbor, where a man named John Lindsay had taken him in and seen him through to graduation. He claims that one of the few things he remembers his mother telling him was that he was born in California. With that information and his birthdate, he was able to acquire a birth certificate and has thus come to Luna Bay in search of information about his father—the Oedipal search that is a major theme in Macdonald's works.

Archer recognizes some crucial flaws in the boy's story. The orphanage is said to have burned down leaving no records, John Lindsay is dead, and, as Archer says, "Birth certificates are easy to get ... you can write in, pay your money, and take your choice."

To resolve the question of the boy's authenticity, Archer flies to Ann Arbor to do his own research. He discovers there that the boy had been a very fine actor and had had one very good offer from "some big producer" who "wanted to give him a personal contract and train him professionally." From an old girlfriend, Ada Reichler, he discovers that:

> The poor damn silly fool was born and raised right here in Ontario. His real name is Theodore Fredericks, and his mother runs a boardinghouse in Pitt, not more than sixty miles from here.

At this point, things obviously do not look good for young Mr. Galton/Brown/Fredericks. But as more information is sifted and pieced together, enough facts are uncovered to prove that he really is the missing heir, the true son of Anthony Galton/John Brown.

The circumstances which are brought together to confirm this story demonstrate Macdonald's masterful plotting. We must first recall Peter Culligan, Gordon Sable's houseman, slain in the early pages of the book. Culligan was at Luna Bay at the same time as Anthony Galton/John Brown, Sr. and Culligan knew of Brown's family wealth through his wife, the Brown's nurse. When the boy, John Brown, Jr., was 16, Culligan ran across him at the boardinghouse in Canada while visiting his old friends, the Fredericks, and began to plot to get him back to California to use him to get money out of his grandmother. But Culligan was not sharp enough to handle the swindle alone. Through a coincidental meeting with Sable's wife, Alice, in Reno, he discovered that Sable was the Galton's attorney and began to plot with him toward getting a part of the boy's inheritance. Sable was the "big producer" who had gone to Ann Arbor to enlist the boy in the scheme.

In the final resolution of the plot, two murders are explained. The first is that of Peter Culligan. Suspicion shifts from a minor character, Tommy Lemsberg, to Sable's wife, Alice, and finally comes to rest on Sable himself. As he explains:

> I had to kill him. You don't seem to understand. . . . He kept moving in on me. He wasn't content to share my wife and my house. He was very hungry, always wanting more. I finally saw that he wanted it all to himself. Everything.

In the final chapter, we get an explanation of the murder of Anthony Galton/John Brown, Sr. Anthony/John, Jr., had been told by Culligan that his stepfather, Nelson Fredericks, was in fact the man who had killed his real father. He finally confronts his mother with this information and accuses her of helping him or at least of helping him cover it up. Under the pressure of the investigation, Fredericks commits suicide and the mother is at last free to explain:

> I saw him cut off your daddy's head with an ax, fill it with stones, and chuck it in the sea. He said that if I ever told a living soul, that he would kill you, too. . . . He held up the bloody ax over your crib and made me swear to marry him and keep my lips shut forever. Which I have done until now. . . . For sixteen years I stood between you and him. Then you ran away and left me alone with him. I had nobody else left in my life excepting him. Do you understand what it's like to have nobody at all, son?

Surely there are themes here typical of Macdonald. The initial murder, of Anthony Galton/John Brown, Sr., was committed by Fredericks because he wanted Galton's wife and money. And the scheming which brings down Peter Culligan and Gordon Sable constitutes a greedy attempt by those outside the affluent society to defraud those within it. It is particularly ironic to recall that Anthony Galton left home with a vision of a new civil war between the rich and the poor, a feeling that his money "cut him off from life," and a desire "to get *closer* to America." He, in fact, found himself among the cruelest, most disenchanted element of that civil war, was cut off from life at least partially *because* he had the money which they wanted, and got so close to America that his bones were turned up in the dust of excavation for a new shopping center as the country plowed obliviously into the future. Events suggest that it is no easier or safer to attempt to bridge that gap between the haves and have-nots than the original John Brown, of Harper's Ferry fame, found it in 1859.

Another theme stressed heavily in the book is that of personal alienation, of individuals cut off from each other without communication, without friendship. Mrs. Galton at 73 has spent the last ten years of her life in the same room of her mansion. Her son Anthony chose to isolate himself from his own past and did not long survive. Sable, as part of his rampaging explanation of his actions, says "I have no friends" and then speaks of himself and his wife acting out their feelings "like clowns, or apes in separate cages." And finally, there is the mother, Teddy, "past comforting," lamenting the sorrowful state of her affairs with "nobody else left in my life excepting him" and asking her son: "Do you understand what it's like to have nobody at all, son?"

The most obvious parallel to Macdonald's own life in the book is the physical circle it closes in the travels of John Brown, Jr., from birth in California to childhood and adolescence in Canada to schooling in Michigan and the final return to California. It is interesting to note the passage in which Archer finds a suitcase in Peter Culligan's room following his murder. On opening it, he notes that its "contents emitted a whiff of tobacco, sea water, sweat, and the subtler indescribable odor of masculine loneliness." In the same essay in which he tells the story of his grandson Jimmie, Macdonald has said of this passage that

> these were the smells, as I remembered and imagined them, of the pipe-smoking sea-captain [his father] who left my mother and me when I was about the age that grandson Jimmie was when he became a monster . . . and then a laughing boy, and fell asleep.

The importance of the sea and sea-imagery in Macdonald's works will be discussed in Chapter 6, but here we can see that part of Macdonald's fascination involves his own father search. We may well imagine that just as grandson Jimmie feels irrational fears and blames himself and the monster within him for his parents' apparent desertion, so might the young Macdonald blame himself and his own monster for the desertion of his father. Or put another way and given a broader thematic brush, Macdonald relates similar feelings to his own hard times during the Depression in Canada (after his high school years) as a pauper cut off from his birthplace and natural home in the imagined paradise of California:

> In a puritanical society the poor and fatherless, suffering the quiet punishments of despair, may see themselves as permanently and justifiably damned for crimes they can't remember having committed.

Macdonald sees such family pressures as the desertion of a parent and such socio-economic pressures as the Depression as tending to widen the basic Platonic split between the ideas of more worthy and less worthy substances. In the mind of a child, such splits foster a sense of hopelessness and despair. He says of *The Galton Case* that it "was an attempt to mend such gross divisions on the imaginative level. It tried to bring the Monster and the Laughing Boy into unity or congruence."

Macdonald recalls that the initial conception of *The Galton Case* appears "abruptly, without preparation" in one of his spiral notebooks as simply: "Oedipus angry vs. parents for sending him away into a foreign country." He explains that:

> This simplification of the traditional Oedipus stories, Sophoclean or Freudian, provides Oedipus with a conscious reason for turning against his father. . . . It re-reads the myth through the lens of my own experience, and in this it is char-

acteristic of my plots. Many of them are founded on ideas
which question or invert or criticize received ideas and which
could, if brevity were my forte, be expressed in aphorisms.

The myth which is *The Galton Case* provides its Oedipus
(John Brown, Jr.) with two fathers—one killed at the hands
of the other—and makes its ultimate statement in terms of
characters' relationships to the past and the human violence and tragedy buried there.

Mrs. Galton has been living in one room of the past for
ten years. Only when faced with the certainty of her own
death is she motivated to come to terms with the present
and the future. Whether her real motivation is "forgive-
ness" or a brand of selfishness desiring to perpetuate itself
through its rightful heirs is moot; the impetus is there. Her
son, Anthony Galton/John Brown, Sr. sought to slough off
the burden of the past in a single gesture and found himself
entangled in an element of the present with which he was
unprepared to deal. His life came to a violent end. Nelson
Fredericks committed the horrendous act of murder in the
wild present in which he lived in 1936 and then tried to stop
time by spiriting his "adopted" family away to the frozen
North. But past deeds and an unavoidable present finally
conspired to complete his destruction.

At the end of the novel, however, we are offered a faint
ray of hope. John, Jr. has made a thorough examination of
his past but is not bound by it. He has found a girl, Sheila,
whose innocent, uncritical faith in him is ultimately justi-
fied despite Archer's initial skepticism. As they leave the
boardinghouse in the final scene, the river is flowing, the
trees rustling and the birds singing. About this ending, Macdonald has remarked that the "morning birds appear there
as reminders of a world which encloses and outlasts the
merely human." There is hope—that a younger generation
may survive the horrors of the past and live in a peaceful
present toward an optimistic future. Nature, at least, will
not succumb to the merely human, voracious appetite for
destruction.

*The Ferguson Affair* (1960) marks Macdonald's second desertion of Archer in favor of another protagonist. The narrator here is Bill Gunnarson, a married lawyer with a pregnant wife. Though the novel lacks the controlling unity of the single family saga which characterized *The Galton Case*, family relationships do inform the book's thematic substance.

The central character is Colonel Ferguson, a Canadian oil millionaire who has married the American Dream, a ravishing blonde starlet risen from humble circumstances. Her family, the Doterys, is dominated by a raging, self-pitying, money-hungry father. Another family which we glimpse is that of Harry Haines, who is described as "self-conceived out of nothing, a fatherless man with a gun, trying to steal reality for himself." His husbandless mother lives in a total fantasy world. Finally, the narrator, Gunnarson, has his own family; we see him alternately torn between his duty to the case and his duty to his wife and unborn child.

As in *Meet Me at the Morgue*, it is interesting to consider the author's possible reasons for abandoning his proven narrator, Archer. The motivation seems similar. With the portrayal of a female counterpoint to the narrator's masculine concerns and with the birth of a child in the course of the novel, Macdonald is dealing again with situations into which Archer's character would not comfortably fit.

*The Ferguson Affair* attempts to control a widely divergent set of plot lines. The intrigue of organized crime, mysterious hospital-related deaths, the curious lives of movie stars, a wealthy Canadian awash in this new land, suspected police corruption, the truth of family relationships buried in the past, and an underlying domestic subplot are combined in the complex story line. Critic Peter Wolfe, in *Dreamers Who Live Their Dreams: The World of Ross Macdonald's Novels*, feels that "because the book has too much material, some of these things lack definition" and finds the ending "clogged and contrived." But despite a lack of unity, the novel does contribute new insight into basic themes.

Significantly in this work, a new sympathy is created for

the wealthy victimized by wealth. Colonel Ferguson is a Canadian from Alberta whose fortune was made by the discovery of oil on the family property. His father died poor and Ferguson has never mastered his own feelings of guilt and inferiority over his belief that his father "was a better man than I shall ever be." In a startling image associated with his return to Canada for his mother's funeral, we read:

> The gravediggers had to use pickaxes and blowtorches to break through the crust of the earth. The lake below the graveyard was nothing but a flat place under the snow. The wind swept down from the Arctic Circle across it.
>
> They covered the chunks of frozen earth with that imitation green grass they used in those days: a little rectangle of horrible fake green in the middle of the flat white prairie, with wooden oil rigs standing on the horizon.

Ferguson here witnesses the reality of his own mother's death glossed over by a little patch of fake greenery in the frozen prairie, as the oil wells, symbols of the emotionless technology and his own future wealth, continue their mechanical production of his own moral destruction. He uses some of his earnings from his initial windfall to buy off his guilt over having gotten a girl pregnant in Boston, but he does finally recognize and admit in the end that money has "been a root of evil in my life." Gunnarson remarks that "he was one of those victims whose natures, whose whole lives, set them up for a particular crime." The remark is in the context of the crime of extortion, but there is a larger sense in which Ferguson's whole life, following the discovery of oil, is the story of a man victimized by the systematic forces of technology, the arbitrary wealth it produces, the human weaknesses that succumb to that wealth and the external forces of greed and envy which play upon it. Ferguson is the first major character of wealth for whom we have seen Macdonald create such sympathy. The distinct political and moral lines based strictly on wealth begin here to blur.

Sympathy also accrues to Ferguson because of certain analogies between him and the narrator Gunnarson. Obviously, they have similar last names, and both men devote their energies to work rather than love and domestic life. Both men have pregnant wives who use the same obstetrician, Dr. Trench.

In the narrator's domestic struggle, we see elements of what were very likely some of the final, divisive arguments between Archer and his former wife, Sue. Gunnarson finally makes it home after midnight to a cold dinner with which his sleepy wife, Sally, has been sitting for hours. Her frustrations burst out:

> You don't want the responsibilities of a wife and family. No wonder you get fixated on your clients. It's a safe relationship, an ego-feeding activity, which makes no demands on your essential self. . . . You're nothing but a profession that walks like a man.

As in *Meet Me at the Morgue*, the question is raised as to where an individual's responsibilities really lie, to family or to mankind? For his part, Gunnarson experiences moments of conscience in the novel when he thinks "to hell with the Ferguson case" and desires only to be at home with Sally looking forward to the birth of their child. That birth appears to set Bill and Sally's relationship on a new course and perhaps offers some insight into the author's choice of narrator in this book. Archer's bachelorhood would have precluded the use of this subplot which offers hope through regeneration and the happiness of family life.

But before pressing too much significance on this blissful resolution, we should recall that in this novel where Gunnarson gains a daughter, Ferguson loses one in a scene that evokes the absurdity and horror toward which family relationships can lead. And only two novels previous, in *The Doomsters*, Mildred Hallman proved that pregnancy and childbirth were not a panacea for domestic ills. It is through the yoking of such contrasts that Macdonald attempts a portrait of the full range and shading of human experience. Significantly, this novel demonstrates his continuing concern to articulate the positive, if complex, notes absent in the earlier books.

Though *The Wycherly Women* (1961), like *The Ferguson Affair*, offers certain optimistic forecasts, greater attention is paid to rendering the ambiguity of evil. Macdonald takes the word *blame* as a focus for this concern and various references to *blame* create a resonant chord throughout the book.

In an early passage, Archer is speaking with Dolly Lang, the roommate of Phoebe Wycherly. Dolly is studying sociology and falls into a discussion with Archer about whether parents or children are responsible for juvenile delinquency. Archer avoids taking sides by saying he doesn't blame anybody:

> I think blame is one of the things we have to get rid of. When children blame their parents for what's happened to them, or parents blame their children for what they've done, it's part of the problem, and it makes the problem worse. People should take a close look at themselves. Blaming is the opposite of doing that.

The conversation is a significant development of the guilt theme. Blaming is a way of placing guilt outside oneself. Archer suggests that the place to look is inside.

As he leaves Dolly, Archer notes the last unfinished sentence of the sociology term paper she has been typing: "Many authorities say that socio-economic factors are predominate in the origins of anti-social behavior, but others are of the opinion that lack of love...." Though couched in the abstract jargon of "socio-economic factors" and "anti-social behavior"—which Archer detests—the sentence recalls the "lack of love" theme from *The Doomsters*. The reference is repeated in its entirety a second time in the novel to form a kind of frame for a plot with both too much love of the erotic sort (between Catherine Wycherly and

Carl Trevor) and too little love of the familial sort (between Phoebe and her parents). The statement also allows Archer the opportunity to express his distaste for sociological cant and his concern for language. In an exchange with Bobby Doncaster, Archer explains:

> "You don't want to be a dead loss to the world. You have certain qualities it can use. Courage is one of them. Loyalty is another."
> "Those are just abstract words. They don't mean anything. I've studied semantics."
> "They do, though. I learned that studying life. It's a course that goes on and on. You never graduate or get a diploma. The best you can do is put off the time when you flunk out."

While words may be said to have no meaning in and of themselves, life teaches us that if there is to be meaning at all, we must invest those abstractions with significance and conduct our lives *as if* courage and loyalty and all the great verities do exist. Otherwise, life declines toward murder, chaos, and meaninglessness.

Certain elements of the book tend to argue that Macdonald does not subscribe wholly to theories of decline and disintegration in the world. In a significant passage which illuminates this point, Phoebe is describing a bad night she spent alone in a hotel room. She had been recalling all the bad times of her youth, especially lying in bed at night listening to her parents "quarreling through the walls":

> They never stopped quarreling. They were still quarreling the day she died. I could see them in the dirty window mixed up with my reflection. I could hardly tell if they were in my head or in the night outside, or if *I* was just a reflection in the window, and only those jabbering words were real, whore and crazy and I'll-kill-you. I started to say my name out loud, Phoebe, over and over. It's a name they gave to the goddess Diana in Greek mythology. And the voices went away.

The lack of love which Phoebe experienced in her household threatened her very identity. But, through the link of her own name with a mythological past, she is able to establish a feeling of continuity and to strengthen her sense of self while shutting out the maddening voices and thus steering away from the edge of insanity.

In another classical reference, the tormented lovers in the book are compared to Paola and Francesca, lovers blown ceaselessly about the second circle of hell in Dante's *Inferno*. Such references to classical literature and antiquity draw an historical, mythological matrix beneath the plot. This matrix renders the contemporary story not so much as evidence of an inevitable decline but rather as a demonstration of the endurance of human weaknesses. The proper response, then, to such situations is not fixing blame, but accepting responsibility for the human condition. Personal responsibility assumes a greater thematic importance in Macdonald's later works. Perhaps the suicide at the end of *The Wycherly Woman* can be interpreted as one kind of acceptance of responsibility. But the next novel, *The Zebra-Striped Hearse*, finds a more hopeful image for that acceptance in its resolution.

*The Zebra-Striped Hearse* (1962) is one of Macdonald's cleverest and most involved excursions into the Freudian "family fantasy." The entire murder mystery plot is bound up with the lives of the two remaining members of the Blackwell family, with their attempts to deal with the demands of the family past and name, and with their own stubborn drives to maintain the continuity of the family lineage on the one hand and to break away at all costs into the freedom of individuality on the other.

These two family members are Mark Blackwell and his daughter, Harriet. Mark is another product of war and family neuroses. He is described as

a fairly big man who had begun to lose his battle with age. . . .
His eyebrows were his most conspicuous feature, and they gave him the air of an early Roman emperor. Black in contrast with his hair, they merged in a single eyebrow which edged his forehead like an iron rim. Under it, his eyes were unexpectedly confused.

We learn that Mark is a former career soldier who "only chose that career because it was a family tradition and his mother insisted on it," that he was retired against his will, and that when his first wife, Harriet's mother, divorced him, he was left "with nothing to fill his life but his guns and his sports and the Blackwell family history which he has been trying to write for lo these many years."

Archer describes Harriet upon first meeting her as "a lot of girl" and continues in one of Macdonald's characteristic thumbnail portraits which combine appearance and state of mind:

> She whipped off her glasses, revealing a black scowl, and something else. I saw why her father couldn't believe that any man would love her truly or permanently. She looked a little too much like him.
>
> She seemed to know this; perhaps the knowledge never left her thoughts. Her silver-tipped fingers went to her brow and smoothed away the scowl. They couldn't smooth away the harsh bone that rose in a ridge above her eyes and made her not pretty.

But it is not only this physical mark of the family which makes her "not pretty" that Harriet is fleeing in the course of the novel, it is also the psychological marks. In a conversation with her mother, Pauline, Archer is filled in on Harriet's early life and her relationship with her father. There is also significant information about Mark's relationship with his wife and mother. Pauline says that Mark's mother

> spent the first years of our marriage with us, and I had to sit in the background and watch him dance to her tune. . . . Mark was a little boy in bed. . . . But we won't go into that.
>
> When his mother died, I thought he'd turn to me. I was a dreamer. He transferred his fixation . . . to poor little Harriet. . . . He supervised her reading, her games, her friends, even her thoughts. He made her keep a diary, which he read, and when he was away on duty she had to send it to him. He got her so confused that she didn't know whether she was a girl or a boy, or if he was her father or her lover.
> . . . He conceived the grand idea of turning her into a sort of

boy-girl who would make everything come right in the end for
him. He taught her to shoot and climb mountains and play
polo. He even took to calling her Harry.

This total usurpation of the child's identity by the father
is the proximate cause of the events of the novel.

Initially, Blackwell hires Archer to investigate Harriet's
present boyfriend and prospective husband, Burke Damis.
Blackwell suspects "he's one of those confidence men who
make a career of marrying silly women."

In the course of Archer's investigation, Burke Damis's real
name is shown to be Bruce Campion and two murders are
turned up. One is that of Campion's wife, Dolly. The other
is his close friend, Quincy Ralph Simpson. At first, Campion
is suspected of having committed the murders in an effort
to get close to Harriet's money. She is due to come into a
large trust fund within a year. Suspicion shifts to Blackwell
himself when it is discovered that he was the father of Dolly
Campion's child. Later, suspicion falls on Isobel Blackwell,
Mark's second wife, when it is learned that she knew Dolly
Campion as a child.

Resolution of the plot hinges on what one critic, Bruce
Cook, has called "an astonishing coincidence." When Dolly
Campion was murdered, the murderer took her baby from
his crib and left him in a car next door. The baby was found
clasping a button in his fist that he had pulled from the
murderer's coat. While watching the Blackwell's beach
house one day, Archer notices one of the girls among a
group of beach bums who travel in a zebra-striped hearse.
She is wearing a coat missing a top button that matches the
one found in the baby's hand. The coat had been found in
the surf. When identified, the coat is proven to belong to
Mark Blackwell.

But Mark is not the killer; Harriet is. The truth is that
Mark was one day overcome with guilt about his affair with
Dolly, confessed all to Harriet, and suggested that she go
check on Dolly and the baby (Harriet's half-brother). When
Harriet arrives, Dolly and the baby are out. But Campion/

Damis is there painting and Harriet falls immediately, passionately in love with him. Before long, they are seeing each other regularly. One night Harriet suggests to Campion that she buy him a Reno divorce and that they get married. Campion refuses, saying that he has a commitment to Dolly which he can't break. Harriet is enraged, drives to the Campion house and breaks it for him; she murders Dolly while wearing her father's coat.

Quincy Ralph Simpson then gets involved because he is a friend of Campion and Dolly, because he was aware of her affair with Blackwell, because he recognized the button as belonging probably to Blackwell's coat, and because he fancies himself an amateur detective. When he comes to the Blackwell home one day with coat in hand to confront him, Harriet recognizes the coat, persuades Simpson to go for a ride with her, kills him with an icepick, and buries him in a shallow grave on the site of her stepmother's former residence where she and Dolly Campion played as children. When asked later why she picked that spot, she explains, "It was a safe place. I knew there was nobody there. . . . It kept it in the family."

The final and massive irony in all this is that her father is suspected of both murders throughout most of the book; there is even a time when Harriet has disappeared and he is suspected of killing her. At this point, Archer confronts him at the beach house and accuses him on each count. Blackwell admits to everything, including killing Harriet, and then shoots himself. Archer assumes that the blood in the bathroom is from Harriet's murder, but later discovers that she had, in fact, tried to commit suicide there and that Mark had stopped her. In his final gesture, Mark had tried to be a father to her by accepting the responsibility for his contribution to her shattered life and by trying to arrange things so she could go free. As Archer observes to Harriet:

> he must have known that his affair with Dolly led indirectly to your murdering her and Ralph Simpson. He had nothing to look forward to but your trial and the end of the Blackwell name—the same prospect you're facing now.

In a very real sense, *The Zebra-Striped Hearse* is a chronicle of the end of a family—a symptom of the evil in Macdonald's wasteland. The family no longer exists to provide
coherence and integration into a meaningful, productive
society. Rather, this new world of disjunction and alienation
is a place where the new generation travels in a striped
hearse and sits around bonfires "scattered along the shore,
like the bivouacs of nomad tribes or nuclear war survivors."
As the diner waitress remarks, "You'd think they'd have
more respect, painting a hearse in stripes like that. They
got no respect for the living or the dead. . . . I don't know
what the world is coming to."

But if the end of the family is a symptom of evil, perhaps
the real evil is that the modern world has no clear idea of
evil—a notion Macdonald's mentor Dostoevsky propounds
in *The Brothers Karamazov*. At one point in the story,
Archer consults an art critic, Manny Meyer, in an attempt
to confirm Campion/Damis's identity. Meyer says, "Campion
is a good painter. . . . So good that I don't greatly care what
he did to his wife." Speaking to Archer, he continues:

> You live in a world of stark whites and blacks. My world is
> one of shadings, and the mechanism of punishment is anath-
> ema to me. 'An eye for an eye and a tooth for a tooth' is the
> law of the primitive tribe. If we practiced it to the letter we
> would all be eyeless and toothless. I hope he eludes you, and
> goes on painting.

Archer comments to himself: "He didn't believe in evil. His
father had died in Buchenwald, and he didn't believe in
evil." Clearly, if the son of a man who died in one of the
world's greatest exhibitions of evil does not believe in it, the
world must be in the midst of some great shift from abso-
lutism to a relativism that even Archer finds difficult to
comprehend or accept.

There are no easy explanations, but Archer does make
two brief statements which may be turned on the problem.
At one point, when he is badgering Isobel with his incessant
questions and forcing her to look at the circumstances of

her life and family, he says, "At least you're feeling the pain. . . . It's better than being anaesthetized and not knowing where the knife is cutting you." And elsewhere he speaks of those "who would rather die in a vaguely hopeful dream than live in the agonizing light of wakefulness." Perhaps all we can do is force ourselves to be awake and aware of the pain, to admit that something is wrong. Perhaps that is the first step.

But the book also raises the very complex problem of moral responsibility. We should recall Macdonald's remark that Freud "deepened our moral vision and rendered it forever ambivalent." *The Zebra-Striped Hearse* can be read as a classically Freudian interpretation of the "family fantasy." Harriet feels that her father was stolen away from her by Dolly when she was a little girl. When her father then begets Dolly's child, Dolly becomes a substitute mother-figure to be hated and slain, so that the child, Harriet, can get closer to the father. And since Dolly already has a husband, Bruce Campion, he can be seen as the substitute father which the child strives to possess as her own.

Such interpretations do, indeed, tend to render the question of moral responsibility ambivalent. When we understand the distorted environment in which Harriet's psyche and personal myth were formed, it becomes very difficult to hold her directly responsible for her actions. And when we know something about her father's life and relationship with his mother, it becomes difficult to blame him too severely either. The blame recedes into the shadows of the past. But then much the same can be said for all the directionless youth who wander the shores in zebra-striped hearses with no respect for the living or the dead, for the present or the past, with no clear notion of what to respect: they are natural products of a society out of touch with its own humanity.

The question is of course "What, if anything, can be done about this situation?" Archer suggests that it is first important to feel the pain. And in this work, as in most of the novels, Archer serves a kind of objectifying function. By demonstrating the patterns common to many of the trage-

dies in his version of California, he seeks to persuade people
of the possibility of casting off the guilty cloak of the past
and of boldly accepting a personal responsibility for one's
self and one's environment.

At the end of *The Zebra-Striped Hearse*, Macdonald creates another quasi hopeful and, in this case, striking image.
After a long, beautifully written and psychologically shak-
ing scene in the Mexican church with Harriet, Archer says:

> I put my arm around her shoulders and walked her toward
> the door. It opened, filling with the red sunset. The beggar
> woman appeared in it, black as a cinder in the blaze.
> "What will happen now?" Harriet said with her head down.
> "It depends on whether you're willing to waive extradition.
> We can go back together, if you are."
> "I might as well."
> The beggar held out her hands to us as we passed. I gave
> her money again. I had nothing to give Harriet. We went out
> into the changing light and started to walk up the dry river-
> bed of the road.

Archer, for his part, recognizes where he can be of service
to other people and where he can't; he sees what he can do
and what he can not do. He gives the beggar money. For
Harriet, he can only go with her along the road. She must
take responsibility for her own life and in the meek statement, "I might as well," she takes the first step. The sunset
suggests the end of an old way of life, of the past as Harriet
lived it. The beggar "black as a cinder in the blaze" suggests
the bitter ashes of that past and the end toward which even
Harriet might be shrivelled if she is unable to draw herself
away. But the "changing light" and "dry river-bed of the
road" imply an arduous, but possible avenue toward a new
redemption.

*The Zebra-Striped Hearse* is one of Macdonald's superla-
tive books. Tightly focused, like *The Galton Case*, on a single
family, it marks a new level in Macdonald's achievement. It
is the first book to provide equally sympathetic portraits of
both the older and younger generations. Each suffers the

burden of an oppressive past with which each must make its own reconciliation.

Here, too, Macdonald's creation of a personal mythology takes on new dimensions. Scenes and characters from earlier novels, already a part of the reader's consciousness, are recalled to illumine the story at hand. In a trip back to Luna Bay, for example, where Anthony Galton's bones were uncovered in new excavation, the construction on the site is already declining into dilapidation. Quincy Ralph Simpson's remains are turned up in similar fashion in the wake of construction of a new freeway. Such scenes not only underline the short cycles of obsolescence of contemporary culture and the inevitable death just beneath its surface, but they also weave the threads which draw together the mythology of Macdonald's gradually evolving world.

*The Chill* (1964) was presented the Silver Dagger Award by the Crime Writers' Association of Great Britain. Structurally, the book marks a new level of technical accomplishment. Two plots, which at first seem disparate, are woven masterfully together and shown to have common roots in related calamities. A California academic community provides the setting. The two strands of the plot begin with Dolly Kincaid, a student, and Helen Haggerty, a faculty member.

Dolly is introduced first through her husband of one night, Alex Kincaid. As he explains to Archer, Dolly has disappeared from their honeymoon hotel after a visit from an unknown, bearded man. Within the first four chapters, this mystery is solved. The strange man was Dolly's father and Dolly herself has decided to go back to school. She is supporting herself by acting as driver and companion to Mrs. Bradshaw, the elderly mother of the dean of the college. Dolly has decided she has a life of her own and wants nothing more to do with Alex. From the Dean of Women at the college, Laura Sutherland, Archer learns that Dolly "found out something on their wedding night so dreadful—"

This dreadful revelation must await clarification, but at

the college two literary allusions are raised which serve to broaden the scope of the story—one is to Zeno and the other to Godot. As Archer is standing in a hall, he overhears a bespectacled intellectual female explaning Zeno's story of Achilles and the tortoise to a varisity-sweatered athlete. Achilles can never catch the tortoise, she says, because

> according to Zeno. . . . The space between them was divisible into an infinite number of parts; therefore it would take Achilles an infinite period of time to traverse it. By that time the tortoise would be somewhere else.

The girl tries to explain that "the infinite divisibility of space is merely theoretical," but the boy doesn't get it. Archer stops listening, but the image of Achilles and the tortoise becomes fixed in his mind and recurs as a controlling image for the detective in pursuit of his purpose. The second allusion is to Samuel Beckett's modern masterpiece of tragicomic absurdity, *Waiting for Godot*. Archer meets Helen Haggerty, teacher of modern languges and counselor to Dolly Kincaid, and a bit of literary banter ensues:

> "Looking for someone?" she said.
> "Just waiting."
> "For Lefty or for Godot? It makes a difference."
> "For Lefty Godot. The pitcher."
> "The pitcher in the rye?"
> "He prefers bourbon."
> "So do I," she said, "You sound like an anti-intellectual to me, Mr.—"
> "Archer. Didn't I pass the test?"

The mention of Godot is the second in the novels (the first is in *The Wycherly Woman*) and serves to establish a relationship to contemporary notions of drama, character, theatre, and absurdity in the same way that Zeno marks the classical connection.

Helen Haggerty, Archer's foil in the verbal tryst over Godot, entices him home with her for drinks and conversation. While offering little information on Dolly Kincaid, she speaks of her own fears and of having been threatened over the telephone by an androgynous voice from the past associated with her hometown of Bridgeton, Ill. Despite her trepidations, Archer has the feeling that he is being used and departs.

From a hotel photographer, Archer learns that Dolly's father, Thomas McGee, was convicted of the second degree murder of his wife Constance, Dolly's mother. When he finds Dolly again, she is in the gatehouse at the Bradshaw estate. She has blood on her hands and is hysterical. Alex is present. She says that Helen is dead "and it's all my fault." She speaks of having been "made into a monster" by her father's murder of her mother (we should recall the author's discussion of the monster within us all in "Writing *The Galton Case*") and Archer thinks that she is "performing dangerous stunts on the cliff edge of reality, daring the long cloudy fall." Dolly is put in touch with Dr. Godwin, a psychiatrist she has not seen in ten years.

From Dr. Godwin, we get Dolly's psychiatric history. Her mother first brought Dolly to Godwin when she was ten years old. She was in danger of complete withdrawal. "There's always a good reason," the doctor comments and proceeds to blame her father, "an irresponsible and violent man who couldn't handle the duties of fatherhood." The doctor then explains the circumstances of the mother's death as he understands them. McGee, the father, killed her in "a self-pitying rage" and left the body for the child to find. The doctor had not seen Dolly again because she no longer had a mother to bring her to the office and because her aunt, with whom she then lived, was too busy to make the effort. On the subject of guilt, Dolly's primary motivation, Godwin remarks that "the worst guilt often arises when a child is forced, by sheer instinctive self-preservation, to turn against her parents." He theorizes, along classical psychoanalytical lines, that

> she may well have fantasied her mother's death, her father's imprisonment, before those things emerged into reality. When the poor child's vengeful dreams came true, how else could she feel but guilty?

Parallels between the lives of Dolly and Helen Haggerty are suggested and Archer's mind makes a jump "into blank possibility" theorizing a possible connection between Helen's murder and the murder of Dolly's mother. But despite the extenuating guilt which may have motivated Dolly's actions, evidence continues to mount against her. The murder weapon that killed Helen is found under her mattress, although the circumstances of its appearance there are certainly questionable.

In an interlude that serves to underscore the gap between generations, Alex's father claims that Alex has no connection with the case and tries to take his son home to mother. Archer insults the father ("I don't object to the fact that you're a bloodless bastard. You obviously can't help it") and is fired—but not before he makes his point: "Somebody has to assume responsibility. There's a lot of it floating around loose at the moment. You can't avoid it by crawling into a hole and pulling the hole in after you."

Shortly afterwards, Archer meets Mrs. Hoffman, Helen Haggerty's mother, as she arrives at the airport to handle funeral arrangements. From her he learns that there was a death in Bridgeton when Helen was nineteen that affected her seriously and injured her relationship with her father. The man killed was Luke Deloney, a successful local contractor, aged forty, on whom Helen was said to have had a crush. His death was ruled an accidental shooting, but Helen claimed to know a witness who believed otherwise. Her father was the policeman who handled the investigation and, in her mind, covered it up.

With this information, Archer decides to make the trip to Illinois to follow the leads into the past. There he meets Earl Hoffman, Helen's drunken, despairing father and Bert Haggerty, her divorced husband who "did well in the war ... [but] never ... so well before or since." From them he discovers that Helen's crush was not on Luke Deloney but on an elevator boy named George. And Bert describes a strange rendezvous with his wife and a suspicious couple in Reno the previous summer. The Reno connection, coupled with the fact that Archer saw a car with Nevada plates fleeing the scene of Helen's murder, prompts Archer to make reservations for Reno, but not before making one more call.

He next visits the home of Luke Deloney's widow, one of the daughters of the late Senator Osborne and a lady now past seventy. Her story is that Luke's death was suicide over financial problems, a contradiction of the accepted accidental shooting thesis. "Her eyes flinched, ever so slightly" at the mention of Pacific Point as the place of Helen Haggerty's death. This is the kind of physical giveaway of long-hidden secrets on which Archer's style of detection thrives.

In Reno, Archer locates the man he caught fleeing the scene of Helen's murder and, through him, makes an unclear connection with Roy Bradshaw, dean of the college where Dolly is a student and son of the elderly woman for whom she serves as chauffeur and companion. Following this new twist, Archer locates Bradshaw at the Lakeview Inn in Reno. He finds him there with Dean of Women Laura Sutherland. Bradshaw claims that they have been secretly married for some time and that the concealment of their relationship avoids Laura's having to give up her position under the college's regulations against nepotism. "And then there's Mother. I don't know how I'm going to break it to her," he adds.

Just before leaving Reno, Archer is flipping through *Blazer*, Helen Haggerty's college literary magazine, which he had gotten from her father. It contains a poem by Helen and, as Archer notices, a poem on the light and dark of love signed with the initials G.R.B. Can these be Roy Bradshaw's initials? Can there have been a connection between Helen and Roy twenty-two years ago in Bridgeton?

Back in California, Archer is startled to happen across two elderly women who prove to be Helen Haggerty's mother, Mrs. Hoffman, and the Mrs. Deloney he had just visited in Illinois. Her appearance confirms the suspected link between the murders of Helen Haggerty and Luke Deloney. As Archer follows them out and down the street, he buys a book on ancient Greek philosophy with which to pass the time while they are having lunch. He reads about Zeno and then considers Heraclitus and Parmenides. In *The Dark Tunnel*, we will recall, Robert Branch disputed the Heraclitean notion of flux by suggesting that the integrity of a man was the solid rock in the river. Now Archer says about Heraclitus:

> All things flow like a river, he said; nothing abides. Parmenides, on the other hand, believed that nothing ever changed, it only seemed to. Both views appealed to me.

The aside serves not only to develop the classical matrix but to suggest as well the maturing of the novelist's narrators toward an acceptance of wider possibilities.

In a telephone conversation with his comrade Arnie Walters in Reno, Archer discovers that Bradshaw had been in Reno the previous summer establishing residence for a divorce from a woman named Letitia Macready. For verification of this information, Archer confronts Bradshaw's mother. She is sure Archer is mistaken. According to her, Roy was in Europe the previous summer, and she has cards and letters to prove it. She claims first never to have heard of Letitia Macready, but Archer is convinced that she is lying. Finally she admits that the handsome, "red-headed hussy" had

> picked Roy up on Scollay Square [Boston] and tricked the boy into marrying her. She was in a position to wreck his future. I gave her two thousand dollars. Apparently she spent it on herself and never bothered getting a divorce.

Another talk with Arnie Walters in Reno establishes that Helen Haggerty and Roy Bradshaw knew each other long before the previous summer. And then Dolly's father, Thomas McGee, shows up again wanting to talk. He knows who the other man in his wife's life was. It was Roy Bradshaw. They had both been patients of Dr. Godwin. McGee got his information from Dolly. Dolly's registration in college and her working at the Bradshaw house can thus be construed as an effort to do her own investigating.

Shortly after his conversation with McGee, Archer attends a session at the hospital where Dr. Godwin is questioning Dolly on sodium pentothal. Under the powerful influence of the drug, Dolly recalls the murder of her mother. Her mother was shot by a woman. In the course of an argument before the shooting, her mother called the woman Tish. At the trial, she testified that her father fired the shot because "Aunt Alice wanted me to." And she later claimed to have fired the shot herself "because it was all my fault. I told my Daddy about her and Mr. Bradshaw, and that's what started everything." She says she initially befriended Helen because she thought she might be the woman who killed her mother and she was looking for proof. But then they found that they had much in common and "I told her everything. . . . Helen was killed because she knew too much."

Back at the hotel, Archer talks first with Mrs. Hoffman and then with Mrs. Deloney. From Helen's mother, he learns that Bradshaw was indeed an old school friend of Helen's and that he once went by the name George—George the elevator boy and George Roy Bradshaw, the poet who signed himself G.R.B. When he asks if she ever knew a Letitia Macready, her fumbling hand spills her cup of cocoa. She admits that she is afraid of Mrs. Deloney and that Mrs. Deloney doesn't want her talking about Letitia. When Archer suggests that Tish killed both Helen and Connie McGee, she claims it would have been impossible. Tish was one of Mrs. Deloney's sisters, a daughter of Senator Osborne, and it had been rumored that she was having an affair with Luke Deloney but she "died in Europe when the Nazis ran over France," according to Mrs. Hoffman.

In Mrs. Deloney's cottage, Archer finds that she has a visitor, George Roy Bradshaw. Roy decides to tell the story because "we have to tell someone." As he relates it, Deloney caught him in bed with Tish, became enraged, began hitting both of them with a gun butt, Tish got her hands on the gun, and it went off and killed him. Tish was much older and "the first woman I ever had." His story continues with marriage and a honeymoon in Europe. But his mother had them followed by French detectives; he left Tish in Paris to come home and make peace with her; the war broke out, and he never saw Tish again. Archer is skeptical. Mrs. Deloney produces a French death certificate. But why the Reno divorce if she's dead? Bradshaw changes his story. Yes, he's been leading a double life, dividing his time between mother and wife, but the wife is old and sick now and he has put her on a plane to Rio de Janeiro where he has arranged for medical care. But there are still questions. How did Tish get the gun? Bradshaw is becoming more and more entangled in his own fabrication of the past.

The phone rings. Archer answers. The voice is Laura Sutherland's. Thinking she's talking to Roy, she blurts out, "I'm frightened. She *knows* about us. She called here just a minute ago and said she was coming over." Before Archer can defend himself, Roy knocks him out with a poker and flees.

But Archer is out only briefly and comes to with his eyes focusing on a picture which Mrs. Deloney has by the telephone. It is Mrs. Deloney's father, Senator Osborne. But it matches a portrait in the Bradshaw home which is supposed to be Mrs. Bradshaw's father. Mrs. Bradshaw and Mrs. Deloney are sisters. Mrs. Bradshaw is Tish. Mrs. Bradshaw is not Roy's mother, but his wife.

Archer chases after Roy in his car and catches him just as he has slid his small car across the road to stop another car coming down the hill. The other car is Mrs. Bradshaw's Rolls. Roy has trouble with his seat belts and can't free himself before she crashes into his car and kills him. She continues to claim to be his mother and offers to show his birth certificate to prove it.

Archer has seen too many forged certificates to be impressed and tells her so. He then recounts the unchangeable facts: the killing of Deloney; the marriage in Boston; Roy's falling in love with Constance McGee and the murder that ended it; Roy's finally daring to love again, but managing to convince Tish that Helen Haggerty was the object of his affections; and the final murder which attempted to end that affair. As the novel ends, Tish protests being called old saying, "Don't look at my face, look into my eyes. You can see how young I am." Archer comments: "It was true in a way. I couldn't see her eyes clearly, but I knew they were bright and black and vital. She was still greedy for life."

The Chill is the story of a man who achieves the Oedipal urge to possess the mother-figure and of the consequences of that achievement. The story actually begins with a sexual act more than twenty years in the past. Circumstance turned that act of love into an act of death, the murder of a symbolic father-figure, Luke Deloney. That one death forged a bond so strong that the two people it implicated have lived in a forced isolation of fantasy ever since. Any attempt to break that bond of isolation has been halted by more death.

Although the plot fits a pattern basic to Macdonald's works, it also alters and re-evaluates that pattern. The female, in this case, is greedy for life, greedy for "faithfulness," greedy for power. Her very name, Macready, suggests her all-consuming flaw. It is a role reversal from such relationships as those of Sampson in *The Moving Target* or Professor Tappinger in *Black Money*, who are older men forever seeking to renew themselves with younger and younger partners. From either perspective, the illusion of perpetual youthfulness is a dangerous avoidance of the reality of death. Characters greedy for life, greedy for the illusion of immortality, breed death for those around them.

*The Chill* traces two parallel lives, Dolly McGee Kincaid's and Helen Hoffman Haggerty's. It finally proves the tragedy of each to be rooted in a common past and establishes parallels which reverberate backward through the plot's structure. The Deloney killing, twenty years in the past, set a secondary force in motion. In addition to the bond enforced between Tish and Bradshaw, it triggered Mrs. Deloney's lie covering for her sister and Earl Hoffman's participation in that lie was responsible indirectly for his degeneration as his daughter's contempt for his action alienated them per-

manently. Symbolically, Helen Hoffman "lost" a father.
When Bradshaw's affair with Connie McGee resulted in her
murder, the secondary force of Alice's lie protecting her
sister caused Dolly to symbolically "lose" her father to
prison. When Helen and Dolly come together, their exchange of information comes too close to unmasking the
facts of the past and Helen must die.

Just as Tish's and Bradshaw's roles are a reversal of typical male-female roles in the novel, so is the whole societal
fabric reversed. The motivating, protecting forces seem ma-
triarchal; the men are consistently ineffectual. In a novel
like *Find a Victim*, Macdonald portrays the tyrannizing,
victimizing power of the patriarchal society. In *The Chill*,
there is only one male character of strength, Senator Osborne. But while he only appears in photographs, the dead
patriarch proves to be at the source of the destruction
wrought by his daughters. From him they have acquired
the presumed importance of wealth that lies at the heart of
their ruthlessness. Both operate on the assumption that
money can buy everything: birth certificates, death certificates, silence, happiness. Tish's final proclamation is especially pathetic:

> I was only protecting my rights. Roy owed me faithfulness at
> least. I gave him money and background, I sent him to Har-
> vard, I made all his dreams come true.

In her world, money buys faithfulness and is the stuff of
which dreams are made. Hers is an essentially possessive
love and it is that excessive possessiveness which is responsible for the deaths of Connie and Helen and, very nearly,
of Laura.

Given the enormity of this plot, it is easy to sympathize
with Archer's dilemma whether to accept the Heraclitean
ideas of perpetual flux or Parmenides' perception of stability beneath an appearance of change. There is a sense in
which this story is markedly different from its predecessors.
But beneath the surface there is a sameness in the over-

powering greed and possessiveness bred of money and fueled by illicit sex.

But despite the centrality of the Tish-Bradshaw story, Dolly is the character in the book through which the author makes his statement about the sins of the past visited upon the children of the present. Even before the murder of her mother, Dolly was bordering on total psychological withdrawal from the adult world. Her mental state was a result of her mother's affair with Bradshaw, a weak father-figure, and a tyrannical aunt who devoted all her time to her precious "county work" while the members of her own household were going quietly insane. When the murder disrupted this sinister domestic scene, the innocent child was cut adrift in a sea of unreality. Dr. Godwin makes the observation that there are always good reasons for mental states like Dolly's, but those very reasons can be irrational. In Dolly's case, the central event of her life, her mother's murder, took place at a time when she was still totally under the influence of the "reasoning" of the adults around her, like her Aunt Alice. When she finally realizes that she was wrong in testifying to convict her father, she "reasons" that she is responsible for the violence in the adult world because she relayed information that was the seed of that violence. But her information was conveyed in innocence and in an attempt to reveal the truth. It is the fact that the adults find the truth threatening that is responsible for the violence and responsible for Dolly's confusion to the point that she finally does not know the difference between what happened in reality and what was said to have happened in court. If *reason* has anything to do with the *truth*, there is very little of it in the adult world portrayed in *The Chill*. Rather, *un*-truth manufactures absurdity. And somewhat like the neurotically patient characters in Beckett's *Waiting for Godot*, Dolly waits throughout the book in her own privately absurd world for some adult authority figure to bring reason and meaning to the chaos of her life. Archer serves that function to some extent, but the facts which he pieces together serve more as description of the past than explanation. If there is hope in this book, it is that Dolly has finally been able to bring enough of her unconscious fears and guilts to consciousness so that her future can grow out of a more accurate assessment of the past.

Through allusion to philosophies both ancient and contemporary, the re-writing of the classical Oedipal myth in modern terms, and a plotting technique that weaves roughly parallel stories back to their common root in the past, Macdonald creates in *The Chill* a modern day myth within the rigid confines of the detective format. It is one of his best books.

*The Far Side of the Dollar* (1965) is an inverted, twisted, modern version of the mythical story of Ulysses and Penelope. In the ancient version, Ulysses (Odysseus) and his fellow Greeks have been at war against Troy. But when they finally sack the city, the gods are outraged by the murderous zeal of the Greek soldiers and, particularly, the sacrilege committed against the prophetess Cassandra who is torn from the altar and dragged from the temple sanctuary where she had sought protection. The gods' wrath takes the form of a great storm which strikes the Greek fleet on the way home. Ships and lives are lost. Ulysses loses his way and wanders about the sea and various islands for ten years before he arrives home. He has been away a total of twenty years. But on his return, he finds that Penelope has been waiting faithfully and the story ends with general rejoicing.

In *The Far Side of the Dollar*, the sacrilege also occurs during war and involves a sexual union between the commander of a ship and a sailor's wife as payment to the commander for using his influence to keep the sailor out of jail. But a child is born of this union and the child's attempt in adolescence to establish his true parentage leads to the shattering of the fragile veneer of deception which the adults of this world have constructed to block out the truth buried in the impiety of the past.

But in this contemporary version, there is no lengthy period of retribution imposed by the gods which allows all to come right in the end. The gods are dead and their death marks the essence of the modern world. In this age, retribution for transgressions against the elemental laws of human conduct comes in the form of guilt and psychological anguish. The Penelope in this story ends by stabbing herself with her knitting needles, committing suicide. Her own weaknesses grew largely from her misconceived notions of the power of money. Archer remarks at one point, "She looked at me imperiously, from the moral stilts of inherited wealth," and she says later, "My late father once said that you can buy anyone, anyone at all." Money and sex have come together again to spawn the modern tragedy.

# Mastering the Art

## From *Black Money* to *The Blue Hammer*

> She gave me a long cold appraising look.
> "You really believe that, that everything
> makes sense?"
> "I work on that principle, anyway."
> *The Blue Hammer*

Macdonald's more recent novels achieve a range unequalled
in American crime fiction. From the combination of academic intrigue and international crime in *Black Money*,
through the control of multiple family plots in *The Goodbye
Look*, and the confluence of natural and family disasters in
*The Underground Man*, to the Dostoevskian doubleness of
*The Blue Hammer*, these novels clearly establish the author
as a master of his art. Within the general framework of a
new society being born in post-war California, the author
constructs plots that evolve from the detective tradition but
extend that tradition to confirm the necessity of establishing and expressing values in this technological age. Those
values, no longer externally imposed, are to be found in the
internal commonality of human experience and manifest
their violation in guilt and suffering. Concomitantly, hope
is present in the sympathetic relationships between human
beings conscious of the inevitable horrors and sorrows of
life.

The plotting of *Black Money* (1966) resembles that of *The
Chill* in its doubleness. It entwines two parallel lives of men
from similar slum backgrounds who each finally succumb to
the personal greed at the root of the decadence in Macdonald's world.

Pedro Domingo is a young, very bright Latin American who once stowed away on a boat and jumped ship just off the coast of San Pedro to get to the Promised Land of California. There is some evidence that his grandfather was an educated Parisian named Martel who came to Panama and lost all his money in the canal-building project. This grandfather's wife was supposed to have been a descendant of Sir Francis Drake. With this information, a strong tendency to fantasy, and some pure fabrication, Domingo gets himself accepted into numerous establishment positions. The first of these is as an undergraduate student, without papers, at L. A. State. It is at this point that his path crosses that of the other primary character up from the slums, Professor Tappinger.

Tappinger, or Taps, is a man from the slums of Chicago who worked his way up to a Ph.D. in French and a position at the University of Illinois only to have his world collapse when he was fired for moral turpitude as the result of having gotten a student pregnant. The student is his present wife, Bess, with whom he lives in his current, less-than-ideal position at the local state college.

One of the great ironies of the story involves the circumstances which brought all the major characters together for the first time. Taps once took his wife Bess and a young and beautiful student, Ginny Fablon, to L. A. State to visit his old friend Allan Bosch and to witness a production of Jean-Paul Sartre's *No Exit*. Bosch was accompanied at the play by Domingo, who was, at that time, one of his students and a passionate French scholar.

The play, of course, is a story of hell, which in Sartre's version is three people in a closed room with no windows or mirrors, where there is no such thing as sleep and where the characters are slowly destroyed by their inabilities to tolerate each other. A central line in the play is "Hell is other people" and it applies equally well to the story which Macdonald structures around Taps, Domingo, and Ginny.

During the course of the play, Domingo, in stereotypical Latin fashion, vowed to himself, and later to his landlady, to return someday with a million dollars and a Rolls-Royce to marry Ginny, the girl of his dreams. And also during the play, Bess who was again pregnant, noticed Ginny fondling Taps in the dark. She was overcome with nausea by the recognition of the affair between Taps and Ginny which too-closely paralleled her own affair with Taps some years before, and she left the theatre to throw up.

This incident is far in the past by the time the novel opens at the Montevista Tennis Club near Pacific Point. Much of the action takes place there and concerns its members.

Archer's client from the beginning is Peter Jamieson, whom he describes thus:

> He looked like money about three generations removed from its source. Though he couldn't have been out of his early twenties, his face was puffy and apologetic, the face of a middle-aged boy. Under his carefully tailored Ivy League suit he wore a layer of fat like easily penetrable armor. He had the kind of soft brown eyes which are very often short-sighted.

Jamieson is Ginny's recently jilted fiancé. He hires Archer to check on the mysterious man with whom she is now involved and to try to get her back for him. The mysterious stranger is a man named Francis Martel who arrived only two months previously in a black Bentley and who has been spending vast amounts of money ever since.

In the course of his investigation, Archer learns that Ginny's father, Roy Fablon, died six or seven years before, apparently committing suicide by walking into the ocean. By a bit of coincidence, Archer comes across a photograph of a man named Ketchel (also known as Spillman) who was a big-time Las Vegas gambler staying at the Tennis Club at the time Roy Fablon died. Also in the picture are Ketchel's wife Kitty and, in the background, a more youthful Martel dressed as a busboy.

As leads are traced down and the complications resolved, we discover that Martel is, in fact, the same Pedro Domingo who first appeared at the production of *No Exit*. He has made his dream come true by seizing upon an opportunity that presented itself while he was working at the Tennis

Club as a busboy. He had witnessed there the death of Roy Fablon. The circumstances were such that the gambler Ketchel/Spillman would likely be blamed for the death even though, as it turns out, he was not directly responsible. But Domingo/Martel recognized the difficulty in which Ketchel/Spillman was placed by this death and volunteered to get rid of the body for him. For this service, the boy was taken into the gambler's confidence, sent away to school in Europe, placed in a high position in a Latin American Embassy in Washington, and frequently used as a courier for getting the "black money" out of the country. Black money is the cash which casinos hold back illegally without reporting for tax purposes. It is often smuggled out of the country to foreign, numbered bank accounts and "used to finance about half of the illegal enterprises in the country."

But despite the intrigue of this gambling money story, the murderer is none of these people, but is instead the French professor Tappinger. Taps's fantasy was to be able to extract himself from his present, untenable life and to get back to France with his new love, Ginny, where he could contemplate the "luminous city" of his mind and finally finish the book that he had been working on unsuccessfully for years.

Toward this end, he had been plotting with Ginny. One idea was for her to marry Peter Jamieson, divorce him, take the money and disappear with Taps to France. When Domingo/Martel showed up, their plot shifted to her marrying *him* for *his* money and then proceeding with the divorce-elopement plan.

But the first complication of the Taps-Ginny relationship arose with the arrival of Ketchel/Spillman, who proceeded to get Ginny's father, Roy, heavily indebted to him through gambling. By way of settling up, Ketchel/Spillman offered to take Ginny and do for her much of what he finally did for Martel—educate her, get her in with all the right people, and ultimately use her to his own ends. When Taps learned of this plan, he killed Roy Fablon, partly to forestall this possibility and partly as a result of his irrational rage. When Ginny's mother, Marietta, finally surmised the truth, Taps

had to kill her to cover his tracks. And when Ginny appeared
to be actually falling in love with Martel, Taps had to kill
him, too.

Finally, teetering on the brink of insanity, Taps commits
suicide. In the last paragraph, Macdonald gives us one of
his typical, faintly hopeful resolutions. Returning to the
room where Taps lies dead, he says of Ginny:

> She was lying on the sitting room floor face to face with Tap-
> pinger, their profiles interlocking like complementary shapes
> cut from a single piece of metal. She lay there with him, silent
> and unmoving, until the noise of sirens was heard along the
> road. Then she got up and washed her face and composed
> herself.

There is in that sentence, "she got up and washed her
face and composed herself," the slightest hint that Ginny
may now be able to extract herself from this tragedy,
cleanse her face and spirit, and compose herself for some
more meaningful role, having experienced the tragic catharsis of death and a reflection upon her former corruption.

*Black Money* is another story of the corrupting power of
money and sex. Within the tennis club are people like Peter
Jamieson who have such inherited wealth that they no
longer need deal directly with the community of the outside
world and who turn themselves to gluttony, gossip, prom-
iscuity or gambling to fill up their daily lives. And outside
the tennis club are people like Taps and Domingo/Martel
who long for the leisure of the affluent and who will violate
all moral standards to achieve it. In large measure, it is this
tension between the haves and the have-nots that holds the
story together.

And then there are those, like Jamieson's father, old
enough to reflect for Archer on the longevity of this process
and the unlikelihood of its changing:

> Almost anything can happen here. Almost everything has.
> It's partly the champagne climate and partly, to be frank, the
> presence of inordinate amounts of money. Montevista's been

an international watering resort for nearly a century. Deposed maharajahs rub shoulders with Nobel prize-winners and Chicago meat-packers' daughters marry the sons of South American billionaires.

In this context, Martel isn't so extraordinary. In fact, when you compare him with some of our Montevista denizens, he's quite routine. You really should bear that in mind.

On the nature of the sexual corruption of the society there are three interesting comments in the book. In discussing Taps's behavior with Allan Bosch, Archer comments:

...it's a pattern of behavior that tends to repeat itself. I've had some experience in my work with men and women who can't grow up, and can't bear to grow old. They keep trying to renew themselves with younger and younger partners.

At another point, Ginny says of Ketchel: "Mr. Ketchel wanted everything. Men get that way when they're afraid they're dying." And on entering Ginny and Martel's bedroom after Martel's murder, Archer observes:

The bed, which was its central feature, was circular, about nine feet in diameter. I was beginning to see a good many of these king-sized beds, like hopeful altars to old gods.

In these quotes, one can perceive a statement by the author about the nature of sexuality in the modern world and particularly about how men relate to sexuality. The implication is that a root fear is the fear of death in a meaningless, unstructured world and that men tend to perceive sexuality with ever younger companions as a kind of hopeful, but ultimately empty hedge against death.

In a society where all value is personal greed and aggrandizement, the final outcome is bound to be a grab for wealth at all costs and an infantile refusal to deal with the inevitability of personal death.

*The Instant Enemy* published in 1968 is perhaps the bitterest of the Archer novels and no doubt reflects the violent times of war and student unrest in which it was written and published. It deals more explicitly than any Archer novel to date with marijuana and LSD and employs such period jargon as "escalations and negotiations," "credibility gap," "freaked out," and "blew my mind." Its opening is structured around two teenagers, Davy Spanner and Sandy Sebastian, who are out for revenge against a cold, adult world.

Their actions initiate a series of discoveries of mistaken parentage, assumed identity, and sexual license as complex as any Macdonald has authored. The book's weakness lies chiefly in its development of too many characters, none of whom receives the central attention necessary to evoke the reader's sympathy. It is a case of plot superseding character and the whole of the novel suffering for it.

The book's primary achievement is its creation of a new dimension of operation for Archer. He has a very difficult time gathering information in this book. There is another detective, Fleischer, working on the case who goes so far at one point as to hit Archer over the head and dump him by the side of the road. And Davy Spanner's ex-high school counselor, Langston, also fancies himself a detective and succeeds in muddying the waters of the case. More so than in any of the other novels, people and circumstances conspire to keep Archer from performing his mission.

In the book's first paragraph Archer comments on the morning that "everything looked fresh and new and awesome as creation." By the last paragraph, this optimistic tone has changed radically. He is eating cold chicken and drinking whiskey in his office at night and contemplating the $100,000 post-dated check in his safe which has turned out to be ethically unacceptable. He is contemplating the city out his window, and says:

I had a second slug to fortify my nerves. Then I got Mrs. Marburg's check out of the safe. I tore it into small pieces and tossed the yellow confetti out the window. It drifted down on the short hairs and the long hairs, the potheads and the acid heads, draft dodgers and dollar chasers, swingers and walking wounded, idiot saints, hard cases, foolish virgins.

His initial hope has deteriorated to despondency. It is one of the few times we see Archer feeling defeat at the end of a novel. Times are so bad that even his success at unravelling a very complex case does not satisfy him. Indeed, there is little satisfaction in the human failings he has witnessed. In the end, he is as unable to accept the contemporary world as the drifters beneath his window and is reduced to his private revenge of scattering the wicked money of the evil to the winds.

A front page review of *The Goodbye Look* (1969) in *The New York Times Book Review* by William Goldman signalled new levels of public interest in and critical acceptance of Macdonald's works. Goldman called the Archer books "the finest series of detective novels ever written by an American."

*The Goodbye Look* finds its plot in the interrelated lives of the members of half a dozen families over a period of twenty-five years. But the unity of this book is achieved through its focus on one character, Nick Chalmers, and through its re-working of the tale of Pandora's box.

Archer is called initially to the fashionable home of Larry and Irene Chalmers because an Italian Renaissance gold box has been stolen from the family safe while they were away on a holiday in Palm Springs.

In the early investigation, we discover that the Chalmers have a son Nicholas, whom they appear to be protecting from some unspecified harm, and that Nick is engaged to Betty Truttwell, daughter of the Chalmers's attorney who lives directly across the street.

The gold box, we are told, was given to Mr. Chalmers's mother by an admirer. It contained Chalmers's war letters which he read to Nick as a child in an attempt to impress upon him the manly virtues. Nick, an opponent of the then-current Vietnam war, was not impressed and the letters are obviously a source of some hostility between them.

Suspecting that Nick may have been involved in the disappearance of the gold box, Archer journeys to his university apartment only to find Betty Truttwell there. Betty is
concerned that Nick's "whole life has changed in the last
few days." He has recently been spending a lot of time with
a Mrs. Trask and a man named Sidney Harrow with whom
he has been involved in some curious activities. On the
previous Friday evening while the Chalmers were out of
town, Betty noticed Harrow's car parked in front of the
Chalmers's house. When she went over to check, Harrow
rushed out of the house and abused her. Nick then came out
and knocked Harrow down. They stared each other down at
gunpoint. Betty says, "They had a funny look on both their
faces, as if they were both going to die. As if they really
*wanted* to kill each other and be killed." Archer thinks to
himself, "I knew that goodbye look. I had seen it in the war,
and too many times since the war." Their "goodbye look"
suggests a profound alienation which finds little or no value
in life. We later learn that this scene repeats almost exactly
one more than twenty years in the past.

Archer tracks down Jean Trask in a local motel. He overhears a conversation that suggests she is searching for
her father. When he gets into the room, he finds the gold
box lying on the bed, but since he is "beginning to sense
that the theft of the box was just a physical accident in the
case," he merely offers her advice on securing what is obviously a valuable object and departs to seek out Harrow.
Archer finds Harrow dead in his car in a motel parking lot,
a bullet wound in his head. When he finally traces Nick
down, Nick confesses to having killed Harrow but there are
discrepancies between his confession and the facts of the
case. The lawyer Truttwell suggests that Nick has some
deep-seated psychological problems stemming from an
event that took place when he was eight years old: "I think
he was picked up by some sort of sexual psychopath." But
it is a subject neither the family nor his psychiatrist, Dr.
Smitheram, will discuss.

Lacking any other evidence, Archer traces the gun used
to kill Harrow to Samuel Rawlinson, a retired bank presi-

dent, who purchased it in 1945. He claims to have given the gun to his daughter, Louise Swain, as protection from her estranged husband, Eldon Swain. Eldon and Louise Swain had a daughter, Jean, who is now Jean Trask. Mr. Rawlinson's housekeeper, Mrs. Shepherd, and her husband, Rusty, are other characters introduced here whose lives prove inextricably involved with the case. The Shepherds had a daughter named Rita who appears to have partly caused the break-up in the Swain household. But Eldon Swain's major offense was the embezzling of half a million dollars from his father-in-law's—Rawlinson's—bank. Swain and Rita Shepherd then disappeared to Mexico. We also learn here that the gold box initially belonged to Rawlinson's wife, Jean Trask's grandmother.

When questioned by Archer, Jean explains that her interest in Nick involves his having been a witness to the fact that her father, Eldon Swain, is alive. Nick has identified Swain from a photograph as a man he saw down by the railroad yards when he was a child.

From the police, Archer learns that Eldon Swain was killed in the hobo jungle near the railroad yards in 1954 with the same gun that killed Harrow fifteen years later. Nick's confession of the Harrow killing appears to fit more accurately the circumstances of Eldon Swain's death.

When Archer next follows Jean Trask to her home in San Diego, he finds her dead in the kitchen and Nick Chalmers unconscious in the garage beside several empty tranquilizer bottles. Rusty Shepherd is seen leaving the house. From the emergency room of the San Diego Hospital, Archer calls Mrs. Chalmers, who comments that "life is so strange, it seems to go in circles. Nick was born in that same hospital." Patterns and repetitions begin to overlay each other.

Archer picks up the trail of Rusty Shepherd at Conchita's Cabins, a tumble-down, dollar-a-night motel near the Mexican border. Shepherd has been searching the area for years for the embezzled money which he believes Swain stashed nearby. The proprietress explains that Shepherd had, in effect, sold his daughter to Swain and that that was the initial "business" that brought them together. In a conver-

sation with Archer, Shepherd admits to having driven
Swain to Pacific Point in 1954, but says he backed out of the
deal when Swain began to talk about child snatching.
Archer asks if Swain was a child molester. Shepherd replies:
"Could be. He always liked 'em young, and the older he got
the younger he liked 'em. Sex was always his downfall."

Back at the hospital, Archer finds himself in conversation
with Moira Smitheram, wife of the psychiatrist. He suggests
they have dinner; she suggests they drive to La Jolla. While
strolling on the beach there, she explains that her life has
come round full circle too; she lived on this beach, in a hotel
now torn down, for two years while her husband was in the
war. She shared her quarters with one of her husband's
former patients, a man named Sonny. "Ralph suggested
that I keep an eye on him," she says. "There's an irony for
you." As she tries to walk backwards along the beach, re-
tracing her footsteps, she stumbles into Archer and they
embrace and kiss. Archer is on the verge of his first real
affair in the books, but Moira's actions on the beach suggest
that she is striving to re-capture a vanished past and that
the relationship will be short-lived.

Events and information crowd in. Back at the home of the
now-deceased Jean Trask, we meet her mother, Louise
Swain, again. She confirms that the gold box was given by
her father, Samuel Rawlinson, to his lover, Estelle Chalmers, Nick's grandmother. When asked why the box is so
important, she says: "I guess it stands for everything that
has happened to my family. Our whole life went to pieces."
And she recalls her mother telling Jean and her friends the
story of Pandora's box. They "pretended that was what it
was. When you lifted the lid you released all the troubles of
the world."

Back at the hospital, Archer talks with Nick's mother.
She finally confirms that Nick was missing for a day when
he was eight and that he claimed to have killed a man in
the railroad yards. His parents reacted to the story with
disbelief even after the newspaper verified it the next day.

Archer heads back to Los Angeles to continue his investigation. Since her husband is involved in hospital affairs,

Moira Smitheram goes along as his passenger. They end up at her "rectilinear cliff-top house made of steel and glass and money," which she characterizes as a birdcage for the self. In the course of their sexual encounter, Moira explains to Archer that she left Sonny to return to Smitheram partly because of the guilt her affair engendered and partly for the security which her husband's hundred-thousand-dollar house and four-hundred-thousand-dollar clinic represented. Macdonald's continuing probe of the complex psycho-sexual-economic circumstances which motivate his characters is not gratuitous. Sonny will re-surface shortly as a major figure in the novel. The liaison between Archer and Moira ends with Archer driving away through an early morning fog before Moira is awake. The fog only covers the cliff-top; he drives out of it suddenly and is quickly back into his work routine, on his way to the police station. The fog here, as it does in other places in Macdonald's work, serves to emphasize the hazy, irrational, imprecise aspects of human nature which do not fall readily into the logical patterns generally demanded by the detective format. Though not always obtrusive, that foggy human nature is still there affecting events.

Archer next turns his attention to Betty Truttwell, who has uncovered Mr. Chalmers's war letters which were initially stored in the gold box. While looking over the letters, she recalls for Archer her own irrational fears concerning her recollections of her mother's death in the summer of 1945. Her mother had witnessed a scene across the street at the Chalmers house much like the one which Betty herself witnessed that set the novel in motion. Burglars appeared to be going through the house. When she went to check, they knocked her down in the street, ran over her with their car, and sped away. Any reader familiar with Macdonald's works knows that this parallel crime from the past must contain a seed of the crimes in the present.

The plot edges toward resolution as Archer and Betty realize that the dates on Chalmers's war time letters preclude his being Nick's father. He was at sea in the Pacific when Nick was conceived. Many more of the loose ends from

the past twenty-six years are brought startingly, visually
together through home movies of a swimming party given
by Eldon Swain in the summer of 1943. The movies reveal
Irene Chalmers to be Rita Shepherd, daughter of Rusty
Shepherd and one-time enslaved lover to Eldon Swain.
Larry Chalmers, Irene/Rita's current husband, is also present. He is pictured as always looking over his shoulder "as
if there were pirates behind him," and after he is pushed
into the pool he flounders ineffectually with his eyes closed.
The film ends with a look at Irene/Rita and Eldon Swain:

> As if controlled by a documentary interest, the camera fol-
> lowed the pair as Rita stood spraddled on the diving board,
> and Eldon Swain inserted his head between her legs and lifted
> her. Tottering slightly, he carried her out to the end of the
> board and stood for a long moment with his head projecting
> from between her thighs like the head of a giant smiling baby
> being born again.
> The two fell off the board together and stayed underwater
> for what seemed a long time. The eye of the camera looked for
> them but caught only sparkling surfaces netted with light and
> underlaid by colored shadows dissolving in the water.

The scene marks one of the author's most vivid uses of
water imagery to underscore a basic theme and to move the
plot forward. The idea of men seeking to renew themselves
through ever younger partners is here crystallized in the
grotesque image of "the head of a giant smiling baby being
born again" from between the thighs of a beautiful adolescent. The inevitable end of such perversion is evident in the
symbolic death by drowning. The film runs out and they are
still underwater.

Through a conversation with Irene/Rita after the film,
Archer pieces together the events that set off the present
case. Irene/Rita, Nick's mother, with a desire to "act like a
normal human being," sent one of Nick's graduation pictures
to her mother, Mrs. Shepherd, Samuel Rawlinson's housekeeper. Her father, Rusty Shepherd, spotted it there, took
it to Jean Trask and talked her into hiring Sidney Harrow.
His motive was either blackmail or an attempt to shed new

light on the whereabouts of Eldon Swain's embezzled fortune, or both.

More of the story from the past comes into focus when we learn that Sonny, with whom Moira Smitheram lived in La Jolla, was, in fact, Larry Chalmers. All his war letters were fakes. He had a job in the post office and managed to forward letters to his mother which were copies of Smitheram's letters to Moira. Sonny was the name his mother called him. Chalmers was discharged from the Navy while still in boot camp "for reasons of mental health" and has been living a fantasy life ever since.

In the plot's final resolution, Archer confronts Irene Chalmers concerning what happened to Eldon Swain's embezzled money. She finally concedes that she and Larry Chalmers robbed Swain of the money and staged a burglary in reverse to stash the money in Chalmers's mother's safe. When Mrs. Truttwell came across the street to investigate, she recognized Chalmers and he jerked the wheel of the car which Irene was driving, causing the hit-and-run accident and Mrs. Truttwell's death. Chalmers also killed Sidney Harrow and Jean Trask because "they knew too much about him. He was a sick man protecting his fantasy." By the time Archer reaches Chalmers's house, he has committed suicide. He is found at his desk with his throat cut, wearing a Navy uniform with full commander's stripes. A man whose fragile mental structure was shaped largely by his inability to do the "manly" thing and serve in the war has acted out his fantasy even in the style of his death.

Considering the number of families that Macdonald draws together in *The Goodbye Look*, it is his most ambitious work to this point and succeeds where other works with voluminous material, like *The Ferguson Affair* and *The Instant Enemy*, show weaknesses. It succeeds in part because it is controlled by a concern for one character, Nick Chalmers, who is present throughout the book and whose life and worldly situation is a direct result of all the lives which the plot entwines. Twenty-six years in the past, a man, Samuel Rawlinson, and his son-in-law, Eldon Swain, worked together in Rawlinson's bank. Greed led Swain to commit the white-collar crime of embezzlement. Sexual perversity led him to commit the moral crime of adultery. The instability of a younger man, Larry Chalmers, coupled with the pliability and righteous indignation of a wronged woman, Rita Shepherd/Irene Chalmers, resulted in the highjacking of the embezzler and ended with a death, Mrs. Truttwell's. The sentimental affections of a drunken father, Swain, mingled with ideas of kidnapping, blackmail, and perhaps childmolesting, caused the murder of a father by a son as Nick shot Swain. Fifteen years later, the lingering greed of a peripheral figure, Rusty Shepherd, initiated a series of events that ended with two murders, a suicide, and his own death at the hands of the police. And behind it all is a little gold Florentine box passed from hand to hand since the Renaissance. It is the object which knits the story together and serves to reinforce Macdonald's mythological connections. In the Greek myth, Pandora's curiosity was responsible for unleashing all the plagues, sorrows, and mischiefs in the world. But Pandora was herself a kind of plague, an emblem of the gods' revenge, visited upon men by Zeus because Prometheus in his greed, had stolen fire from the gods and connived a system whereby the gods got only the poorest part of the animal (fat and bones) at sacrifices. Through the creation of Pandora, the first woman, Zeus devised his own clever plan for vengeance against the race of men. Pandora's curiosity was indeed the cause of the plagues, but Pandora's very creation was the result of the greed and cunning of men. The greed and cunning of men is the root of evil in *The Goodbye Look* just as the ancients would tell us it has always been. Macdonald's elaborate plots would seem to argue that there are no new stories, only contemporary versions of old ones.

The evil that exists in the modern world is only the old evil seen through a contemporary prism. And that evil is a manifestation of something basic to human nature which even the myths do not explain. There is a quality of human nature, at bottom, which can only be hinted at, much in the way that Archer hints at Rusty Shepherd's motivations:

The mind that looked at me through his eyes was like muddy water continually stirred by fears and fantasies and greeds. He was growing old in the desperate hope of money, and by now he was willing to become whatever the hope suggested.

At the root of evil exists a hope "sitrred by fears and fantasies and greeds" that men can create something better than the worldly situations in which they find themselves. Such a hope appears as enduring and inexplicable as Man himself. The means of this attempt at self-creation is money. But the end of that usurpation of the creative powers of the gods is untimely, and often violent, death. The story is as old as Prometheus and Pandora, and as current as *The Goodbye Look*.

Critical raves for *The Underground Man* (1971) represented still another level of literary acceptance for Macdonald and his detective novels. A *Newsweek* cover story and a laudatory page one review in the *New York Times Book Review* by Pulitzer prize-winning author Eudora Welty led the acclaim. The book remains Macdonald's most admired and for good reason. It combines an elaborate study of the psychic forces at work within a family with a concern for the power of the natural forces rumbling at the edge of a fragile society. Welty says it "is written so close to the nerve of today as to expose most of the apprehensions we live with."

The story opens with Archer doing one of his favorite things: trying to take the day off. He is awakened by blue jays diving at his windowsill, raucously demanding their customary breakfast of peanuts. In the course of the feeding, a small boy appears at a neighbor's door. The boy's name is Ronny Broadhurst. He and his mother, Jean, are visiting while Archer's neighbors are away. A fast friendship is struck between Archer and the child as they feed the birds, but it is promptly interrupted. The boy's father, Stanley Broadhurst, arrives and accuses his wife of having an affair with Archer. At one point he attempts to strike the child, but Archer intervenes. Finally, Stanley takes the boy with him and departs for Grandma Nell's. Grandma Nell is Stanley's mother, Elizabeth Broadhurst. As they drive away, Archer notes that Stanley is traveling with a young blonde woman.

After a morning of reading the newspaper and paying bills, Archer is interrupted by Jean Broadhurst. She has heard on the radio that a fire is raging out of control near Grandma Nell's in Santa Teresa. Stanley's mother has not heard from him. Jean is worried and persuades Archer to help her locate her husband and son.

On the way to the fire, Archer gets from Jean a capsule summary of Stanley's life and problems. For some time, Stanley has "been looking for his father in the hope that it would put him back together." His father, Leo Broadhurst, ran away with another woman when Stan was eleven or twelve years old. The father search has so occupied Stanley that he barely got through the university, even with the help of Jean's tutoring. And as she adds, "the tutorial relationship persisted into our marriage."

In a brief stop by Stan and Jean's house, two important bits of information surface. One involves Jean's recollection of a story told by the young girl Stan was with to her son Ronny. The girl had been at their house the night before.

> She told him a wild story about a little girl who was left alone all night in a house in the mountains. Her parents were killed by monsters and the little girl was carried off by a big bird like a condor. She said that had happened to her when she was his age.

The second clue comes in the form of a man in a "dark rumpled suit" with a "long pale face" and "cornices of scar tissue over the eyes." He arrives demanding money but will not say why. He is looking for Stan and he calls himself Al.

By telephone, Jean is told that Stan and Ronny and the girl were given a key by Grandma Nell's gardener, Fritz Snow, and that they have gone up to the Mountain House.

Archer's first glimpse of the fire initiates a metaphor of battle between Man and Nature which is continued throughout the book. The battle images develop into an independent subplot and permit the author his boldest and most sustained statement on the alienation between human and natural forces, an essential feature of Archer's California. On this occasion, he says:

> Under and through the smoke I caught glimpses of fire like the flashes of heavy guns too far away to be heard. The illusion of war was completed by an old two-engine bomber which flew in low over the mountain's shoulder ... trailing a pastel red cloud of fire retardant.

At the Mountain House, Archer meets a Forest Service man, Joe Kelsey, who has found Stan. Stan is half-buried in a hole which he appears to have been digging himself. Burn marks indicate that this spot is also the origin of the fire. Stan smoked cigarillos and one appears to have dropped into the dry brush at the moment the fatal blow was struck. A human evil is at the source of the natural holocaust.

Because the wind and fire are rapidly changing direction, Kelsey decides to finish the job of burying Stan in order to protect his body from the fire. Ronny and the girl are missing.

In a visit to the Snows, we get our first close look at the sadly grotesque relationship between the gardener, Fritz Snow, and his mother. Fritz is a frightened overgrown child so unable to cope with the external world that he is very nearly autistic. A part of his psychic problem derives from a physical one, a harelip. His mother is over-protective to the point of belligerence. Fritz finally explains that he let the girl and Ronny take his car because "she let me touch her."

From an acquaintance of the Broadhursts, Mr. and Mrs. Armistead, we begin to get a picture of the missing girl. Her name is Sue Crandall and she has been romantically involved with Mr. Armistead's substitute son, Jerry Kilpatrick, who cares for Mr. Armistead's yacht.

Archer finds Jerry at the yacht harbor. They exchange hostile words. After nightfall, Archer sneaks aboard the yacht and finds Sue and Ronny hiding below deck. His triumph is short-lived. Jerry strikes him over the head with a gun and Archer wakes up beside an empty boat slip. The trio have disappeared and will remain so for a large space in the novel.

Archer continues his investigation by calling on Jerry's father, Brian Kilpatrick. He first comments that he is not responsible for his son's actions and then laments: "We're losing a whole generation. They're punishing us for bringing them into the world." He plays the loving parent helpless at the hands of his ungrateful offspring. But the sudden appearance of a man at the door suggests another view of Kilpatrick. The man is wild-eyed with anger. He has lost his house and everything in the fire. It was a house purchased from Kilpatrick without ever having been informed of the high fire risk known to exist in the area. This initial evidence of Kilpatrick's unethical real estate dealings suggests the philosophical chasm between the idealism of the younger generation and the pragmatic greed of the older. We also learn that Jerry blames his father for his mother's disappearance some years earlier. The sorting out of male-female pairings as they existed in the past and changed over time becomes a major aspect of the plot.

That sorting out must consider relationships over the past two decades. Stan Broadhurst initiated the process himself by placing an ad in the *San Francisco Chronicle* which included a picture of his father and an unknown woman with whom he was believed to have disappeared. He learned from this exercise that his father, Leo, had booked passage for two on a cruise ship for Hawaii, but Stanley was unable to confirm whether the tickets were ever actually used. He also received a letter from a former pastor of a local church who advised:

> Your father chose to leave your mother and you, for reasons which neither you nor I can fathom. The heart has its reasons that the reason does not know. I think it is unwise for a son

to attempt to delve too deeply into his father's life. What man is without blame? . . . The past can do very little for us—no more than it has already done, for good or ill—except in the end to release us. We must seek and accept release, and give release.

Archer considers the advice (borrowed in part from Pascal) to be good, but Stan was obviously unable to accept it and was murdered when his own investigation got too close to facts which others wanted concealed.

Archer's continuation of the case turns up the identity of the woman in the picture with Leo Broadhurst as Ellen Storm, formerly a high school teacher in the area. She is also the ex-wife of Brian Kilpatrick and mother of Jerry. As the various threads of the story come together, we learn that in one year of her high school teaching career her homeroom class included Fritz Snow, the gardener; Al Sweetener, the man who came seeking money from Stan; and a girl named Marty Nickerson. In a display of adolescent bravado, the three of them once stole a car and ran away to Los Angeles with ideas of getting into the movies. Their excursion lasted through three days of sleeping in the car and stealing food before they were caught and returned home. But the real problem was that Marty Nickerson later proved to be pregnant. She was underage. Fritz admitted having carnal knowledge of her and was sentenced to six months in forestry camp. Since the caper to Los Angeles was not Al's first offense, he was sent to Preston prison. Marty married the man from whom they stole the car, Les Crandall, and is now Mrs. Martha Crandall, Sue Crandall's mother. Al got out of prison fifteen years in the past at a time which coincided with Leo Broadhurst's disappearance. He was promptly sent back to prison for theft of government property, Fritz's Forestry Service tractor.

Despite false leads and the tracking down of numerous suspects who later prove to be innocent, the truth of the circumstances surrounding the critical event fifteen years before is finally unfolded. Leo Broadhurst was "the kind of man who couldn't keep his hands off women," at least par-

tially because of his marriage to a woman whose own psychological problems with male ancestors did not permit her
to be sexually responsive—"She was a frozen woman, a
daddy's girl." Leo directed his amorous attention, therefore,
toward several women. His primary interests were Marty
Nickerson Crandall and Ellen Storm. Ellen later explains
that "Martha came to me [her high school teacher] when
she got into trouble.... I interposed my body between
them."

According to Mrs. Snow, Fritz's mother and the Broadhurst's housekeeper, the fateful evening began with a quar-
rel between Leo and his wife over the "woman he had
stashed in the Mountain House." Mrs. Broadhurst had
found out about the steamship tickets. She "went into the
long history of his womanizing" and he turned everything
around blaming her and her frigidity. Leo finally roared off
in his sports car and Mrs. Broadhurst followed him. Stanley
later slipped out of the house and returned with his mother
well over an hour later. Mrs. Snow surmises that Mrs.
Broadhurst shot Leo and that Stanley suspected as much.
"I think the suspicion kept growing on him, but he couldn't
face up to it. He kept trying to prove that his daddy was
alive, right up until the day of his own death."

But Mrs. Snow's explanation of the events is only a part
of the truth. The person who killed Stan Broadhurst was
seen from a distance and described as wearing a wig and
false moustache and beard. Al Sweetener is found wearing
the disguise when he is himself discovered murdered. But
the fake hair pieces are traced to Fritz Snow, who bought
them to hide his physical deformity. In a climactic scene
where Fritz is finally able to muster the courage to do his
own talking, he accuses his mother of being the only person
with access to and reason for stealing his treasured disguise.

Under the weight of accumulating evidence, Mrs. Snow
completes the story. Her original account was true to a
point. Mrs. Broadhurst did follow her husband up to the
Mountain House and caught him there in the midst of in-
tercourse with Martha Crandall. She shot him, but the bul-

let only grazed his skull, leaving him alive but unconscious. The shock of the incident frightened Martha so badly that she ran away leaving her three year old daughter, Susan, alone in the loft overnight. But Mrs. Snow was also present at the Mountain House, and after the scene quieted, she stabbed the unconscious Leo to death and then told Fritz that Martha was responsible for the murder and that he should bury the body deep if he didn't want her to go to the gas chamber. For Fritz, who still idolized Martha, this was incentive enough for him to use the Forestry Service tractor to dig a hole deep enough to bury Leo Broadhurst and his red Porsche. This is the monstrous scene that the child Susan remembers. Mrs. Snow explains her own motives like this:

> You can't call it murder. He deserved to die. He was a wicked man, a cheat and a fornicator. He got Marty Nickerson pregnant and let my boy take the blame. Frederick has never been the same since then.

So Mrs. Snow sees her role as that of avenger against a man she views responsible for her son's neuroses. When Stanley and Al got too close to her secret, her past vengeance had to be protected by more murder in the present.

Al, for one, was always a problem. He was always involved when Fritz got into trouble. He was there the night Fritz took the tractor that got him sent back to prison. But he knew then where Leo was buried and "eventually he came back here hoping to turn his knowledge into money." That desire to convert the guilt and grief of others to money was responsible for re-igniting the embers of the past.

Nevertheless, there is genuine hope in this book. The trio of youthful innocents, Susan, Jerry and Ronny, are finally tracked down and the effort is begun to re-assimilate them into an adult world which is not as they would have it, but which is becoming more recognizably human. For Susan, the re-integration does not come easily. On the way home, she threatens to commit suicide by jumping from the Golden Gate Bridge. She is finally persuaded to accept the world as it exists, partially by the concern of the child, Ronny ("I'm afraid you'll fall"), and partially by Archer's honest agreement that "there is no safe place in the world." But he insists that there is "a safer place" than the ledge on which she stands, tempting the long fall into oblivion, and she finally climbs back over the rail.

In the end, Archer is driving through the life-rejuvenating, fire-quenching rain, wishing Ronny "a benign failure of memory," hoping that his life "wouldn't turn back toward his father's death as his father's life had turned, in a narrowing circle."

*The Underground Man* is Macdonald's greatest achievement because it constructs a world view that incorporates the author's well-honed themes of human pain and suffering within a vast sweep of sympathetic natural forces. When Stanley Broadhurst is killed and buried in a hole he dug himself at the very site where his own father was murdered and buried, the resulting fire erupts almost as a spontaneous natural reaction to the outrage. And when careful, concerned research by Archer, the democratic hero, restores sanity and hope to his psychically injured fellow human beings, the skies open and the healing, renewing rains descend. It is in that rain and in Archer's friendship with the child, Ronny, that the author finds his most powerful symbols for the expression of an optimistic declaration on the future. And it is in this book that he achieves his strongest statement concerning a meaningful relationship with the past: "The past can do very little for us . . . except in the end to release us. We must seek and accept release, and give release."

Calling *The Underground Man* Macdonald's greatest achievement is in no way to depreciate his next novel, *Sleeping Beauty* (1973). *Sleeping Beauty* opens with one of the author's most evocative similes. Archer is flying into Los Angeles from Mazatlan and gets his first glimpse of the oil spill which serves as controlling symbol of this book: "An offshore oil platform stood up out of its windward end like the metal handle of a dagger that had stabbed the world and made it spill black blood."

The plot of the novel traces the history of families, primarily the Lennox family, over three generations to provide a composite portrait of the human malice and greed which have finally erupted to pollute the natural order. As in *The Underground Man*, the relationship between the human and natural orders is portrayed as a very fragile one in which subjective human evil is almost mystically objectified in nature. But as in all of Macdonald's works, the primary concern is the human pollution welling up out of the past to endanger the present.

The Lennox Oil Company is the corporate entity responsible for the spill. The Lennox family which operates the oil company is descended from the great patriarch William Lennox and his wife Sylvia. The family has operated under the principles of "what's good for the company is good for the family" to the extreme of marrying a daughter, Elizabeth, to Ben Somerville because he was in a position to insure that the Navy bought Lennox oil during the war.

The men of the family continue to treat the women like toys or property down to the present day. The founding father himself, William Lennox, is in the process of divorcing his wife of fifty years to marry a woman half his age. It is hardly surprising, then, that the person responsible for the killings in the book should prove to be a woman, or that she should lament: "Why should I be the only one to suffer? You men have all the fun. And then you leave the women alone to suffer."

As Archer goes in the final chapter to confront the killer, he is watching the workboats and men on the shore as they spray the slick with chemicals and gather the oil-soaked straw to burn on the once-pure beaches. In a comment typical of Archer's own complex humanity, he thinks, "I envied the men on the boats and on the beaches. I envied anyone who didn't have my errand to perform." And after the killer has leaped to her death from the cliff, we read that "smoke swirled over her body like the smoke from funeral pyres." In the final image, the human and natural tragedies are forged into a vision of unity. It is an image of death and destruction, but it is also true that the men working on the beaches demonstrate a social determination to clean and renew and up on the cliff the beautiful daughter is asleep and alive. Purged of the past, she at least has a chance to awaken to a saner world.

*Sleeping Beauty* is a powerful book. Successful in its demonstration of the equivocal nature of evil, the novel also succeeds in portraying the ambiguity of hope. It does so through the predicament in which it places Archer at the end. Throughout the novel he has had an inordinately high erotic interest in the daughter, Laurel. In the end, it is his excessive attention to the sleeping Laurel which allows the murderess her opportunity to commit suicide. Archer's own imperfections recall a more general imperfectability and the need to accept the world as such. If this ending makes Archer a failure, as Peter Wolfe suggests, his failure must be seen as a reflection of the failure of humanity; concern for the self, the ego, is always present to challenge the altruistic impulses. The dichotomy between Self and Other is an affliction of the modern mind, a doubleness with which Macdonald deals throughout his works and one to which we cannot expect Archer to be immune.

*The Blue Hammer* (1976) continues to probe the complexities of Archer's humanity and does so within the author's most carefully constructed plot on the theme of doubleness. Its time-space frame begins in 1943 in Arizona. Two half brothers, William Mead and Richard Chantry, both painters, are presumed to be sons of wealthy copper magnate Felix Chantry. Mead has the better reputation as a painter, but he has been drafted into the war. In his absence, Chantry, who managed to avoid the military, has stolen some of Mead's paintings, representing them as his own, and has married Mead's former girlfriend, Francine. Mead, meanwhile, has been forced into a marriage with a woman by whom he has had a child. While home on leave, Mead kills Chantry, switches clothes with him and leaves his body in the desert. By the time the body is discovered, it is nearly unidentifiable. With the cooperation of Mead's mother it is mistakenly identified as Mead himself. Mead is then free to

assume Chantry's identity, which he does. The switch gets
Mead out of both a bad marriage and the military and allows
him to start a new life with his former lover, Francine, in
California. Within a short time he establishes himself as an
artist of the first rank and spends seven relatively blissful
years in his self-created world. But on July 4, 1950, he deserted the dream.

He makes his own explanation in a farewell letter that
speaks of his "need to discover new horizons beyond which
I may find light that never was on sea or land" and continues:

> I must seek elsewhere for other roots, a more profound and
> cavernous darkness, a more searching light.... For it is not
> just the physical world I have to explore, but the mines and
> chambers of my own soul.

Copies of the letter are sold at the local museum and Chantry's memory (sentimentalized) supports the romantic fantasies of the local cocktail circuit.

In the present time of the novel, a new Chantry painting
emerges, is subsequently stolen, and Archer is brought into
the case to find it. Circumstances bring him to be primarily
concerned with the Johnson family. Jerry Johnson, the father, is a degenerate drunk who is kept locked up in his
house for his own protection. His wife is a coldly aloof, neurotic personality who has trouble holding nursing jobs because she has been accused of stealing drugs. Their son,
Fred, is a confused, displaced, perpetual student of about
thirty who works part-time at the local museum. We learn
that Fred initially took the painting in question from the
home of the Biemeyers, Archer's clients, with the intention
of proving or disproving its authenticity for himself. But,
according to his story, someone then took it from him. We
also learn that Fred's interest in the painting has something to do with his belief that he is not Johnson's son.

In the course of searching for the missing painting,
Archer meets a young newspaper reporter, Betty Jo Siddon,
who is also working on the Chantry case. This device pro-

vides Archer with both a professional associate and a romantic interest, complicating his life with the double pull of love and work. When Betty subsequently disappears while pursuing leads, Archer is torn between his conflicting desires to locate her and to follow the Chantry case.

But the man who exhibits the most complex doubleness is the painter William Mead/Richard Chantry himself. The truth about Mead/Chantry and his mysterious disappearance is finally resolved. He was visited in 1950 by his wife and child from his army days accompanied by an old army friend. They are the only people who can blow the whistle on his ruse. His solution, bizarre on its surface, is to kill his army friend and to return to his former wife and child. That wife and child are Mrs. Jerry Johnson and Fred. William Mead, who left the farewell letter speaking of his search for "a more profound and cavernous darkness, a more searching light," has spent his last 25 years becoming Jerry Johnson, the shrivelled old, drunken recluse in the attic at the mercy of his wife, whom Betty Siddon describes as

> one of those wives who can watch a man commit murder and feel nothing. Nothing but her own moral superiority. Her whole life's been devoted to covering up. Her motto is save the surface and you save all.

The story describes a curious circle. The imposture actually started with the real Chantry's theft of Mead's paintings and girlfriend. First Chantry pretended to be Mead. But then the real Mead murdered the pretender and assumed Chantry's identity. Mead next moved with Chantry's ex-wife to the town where his own abandoned wife and son resided. Archer surmises that:

> It may be that his living here, so close to his wife and son but invisible to them, was part of the game of doubleness he was playing. He may have needed that kind of tension to keep him in orbit and sustain the Chantry illusion and his art.

What Mead actually had on his mind, of course, his real motivations, will never be totally discovered. We can only see the results of his choices and the quarter century of suffering to which he has submitted, presumably in atonement for his sins.

The question of choices is shown to be a difficult one in *The Blue Hammer*. Francine Chantry complains, as others have throughout the novels, that she had no choice in how her life turned out. Archer suggests she made her choices long ago. But William Mead's decisions are much harder to dispute. Like everyone else, he had no choice about his birth, but his conception was under especially inopportune circumstances—as his father says, "just one of those accidents that happen to people.... after a high-school football game." His first irreversible choice was to kill Richard Chantry, but that was bound up with considerable provocation and mitigating circumstances, the man was virtually stealing his identity. His second irreversible choice was to kill the original Gerard Johnson, his old army buddy, and return to his former wife and child. But that choice too was under the pressure of overpowering circumstance and atoned for over twenty-five psychologically torturous years. It is surely a story complexly enough construed to make us wonder with Betty Siddon "if certain things aren't fated" and to respond with Archer, "Of course. By the place and time and family you're born into. Those are the things that fate most people."

Consistently in these later novels, the author demonstrates the consequences of lives lived without a concern for the simplest values, without regard for the effect of an individual's egoistic actions on his or her follow human beings. Tappinger, Ketchel/Spillman, Larry Chalmers, Eldon Swain, Leo and Stan Broadhurst, and William Mead, to name the most obvious cases, are all characters unable to see beyond the crippling limits of their own selfish fantasies and greeds. Though all of them have suffered under massive mitigating circumstances, their failing, finally, lies in their refusal or inability to accept personal responsibility. But, though these books chronicle the demise of valueless characters, they also delineate the discovery of value. The discovery is frequently made by the younger generation. Ginny Fablon, Nick Chalmers, Brian Kilpatrick, Sue Crandall, and Ronny Broadhurst all see the outcome of the shortsighted motivations of their elders graphically demonstrated. With Archer's help, they also comprehend more positive possibilities for their own futures in lives lived with compassion and a concern for personal relationships.

William Mead, in *The Blue Hammer*, completes the journey through all the blind alleys of selfishness to emerge finally on the brink of self-discovery. In the resolution of that book, value is shown to lie in self-knowledge and in the expanded awareness of the communally shared weaknesses which that self-knowledge enlightens.

# Lew Archer

## The Democratic Hero

I'm just a type.
*The Zebra-Striped Hearse*

Ross Macdonald has said of his detective, Lew Archer, that he is "a deliberately narrowed version of the writing self, so narrow that when he turns sideways he almost disappears." While we may agree that Archer is not the primary object of attention or the "emotional center" of the books, we should also consider that Macdonald has called him "the obvious self-projection which holds the eye (my eye as well as the reader's) while more secret selves creep out of the woodwork behind the locked door." Certainly close attention to all the bits of information provided about his life through eighteen novels and a collection of short stories gives Archer sufficient depth to be in little danger of disappearing and offers significant insight into the author's intentions and purpose.

An analysis of Archer's life, style of detection, and significance in the over-all design of Macdonald's work should first place him in historical context. His name does that for us; it is taken from Miles Archer, Sam Spade's murdered partner in Dashiell Hammett's *The Maltese Falcon*. But, though the name alludes to Hammett, Macdonald sees his character as "patterned on Chandler's Marlowe," another "semi-outsider. . . fascinated but not completely taken in by the customs of the natives."

While Archer is an admitted outgrowth of Macdonald's two acknowledged masters, Hammett and Chandler, he also serves the function of critiquing the style of his predecessors. In his essay "The Simple Art of Murder," Chandler wrote:

> In everything that can be called art there is a quality of redemption. . . . But down these mean streets a man must go who is not himself mean, who is neither tarnished or afraid. . . . The detective in this kind of story must be such a man. He is the hero, he is everything. . . . He must be the best man in his world and a good enough man for any world.

While Macdonald greatly admires Chandler's novels, he strongly objects to this simplistic analysis, pointing out that while

> there may be a "quality of redemption" in a good novel, it belongs to the whole work and is not the private property of one of the characters. . . . The detective-as-redeemer is a backward step in the direction of sentimental romance, and an over-simplified world of good guys and bad guys.

Archer is not a redeemer, but he is a man of the streets and to comprehend him and the place he occupies in his world, we must first look at his life. Early information is sketchy but significant. He is a Gemini, born on June 2 of an unspecified year. (June 2 was the wedding date of Kenneth and Margaret Millar.) By the time he makes his first appearance in a novel, *The Moving Target* (1949), he is 35 years old. Born in Long Beach, he evidently experienced several moves as a child. He went to grade school in Oakland. From his days at Wilson Junior High (city unspecified) he recalls a female vice-principal "who disapproved of the live bait I used to carry in the thermos bottle in my lunch pail, and other ingenious devices." And he recollects many Saturday afternoons of his childhood spent in movie houses where he was a fan of Raymond Campbell's serials; "His Inspector Fate of Limehouse series. . . helped to make me a cop, for good or ill."

There are limited bits of information about his relatives. In *The Chill*, a plaque on a wall ("He is the Silent Listener at Every Conversation") brings back memories of his grandmother in Martinez who "had hand-embroidered the same motto and hung it in her bedroom. She always whispered." In *The Drowning Pool*, a reference to uncles prompts the memory that "I myself was the nephew of my late Uncle Jake, who once went fifteen rounds with Gunboat Smith, to no decision." And in a rare allusion to his parents, he recalls "the day my father took me to San Francisco for the first time" and that his mother never kept any pictures of Uncle Jake "because she was ashamed to have a professional fighter in the family." In *The Goodbye Look*, La Jolla evokes fond memories of surfing in the area during his adolescence. He remains, like his creator, a good swimmer.

Archer is thus a solidly American product reared on Saturday afternoon serial fantasies amidst a world of masculine pugilism, feminine gentility and whispered religiosity. Perhaps the most significant omission from this sketchy early history are facts relating to his parents. The silence, taken together with his frequent moves in childhood and the obvious parallels with the author's life, suggests that he, too, was the product of a broken marriage, a fact that may serve as partial explanation for his own marital difficulties.

But between his fairly typical childhood and his maturing as a soldier, policeman, private investigator, lies a period of angry adolescence bordering on the sociopathic. The most complete revelation of this period comes in *Find a Victim*. Bozey, a petty thief whose crimes have finally mushroomed out of his own control to spread death and destruction across the Southwest, has been interrogated, and "worn down under the padded blows of words [until]. . . . he had nothing left but a stubborn mulish terror." Archer sympathizes with that terror:

> I sweated with him, trying to guess the life behind the record. I had lifted cars myself when I was a kid, shared joy-rides and brawls with the lost gangs in the endless stucco maze of Los Angeles. My life had been like Bozey's up to a point. Then a whisky-smelling plain-clothes man caught me stealing a battery from the back room of a Sears Roebuck store in Long

Beach. He stood me up against the wall and told me what it meant and where it led. He didn't turn me in. I hated him for years and never stole again. But I remembered how it felt to be a thief. It felt like living in a room without any windows. Then it felt like living in a room without any walls. It felt as cold as death around the heart, and after a while the heart would die and there would be no more hope, just the fury in the head and the fear in the bowels. Bozey. But for the grace of an alcoholic detective sergeant, me.

In *The Doomsters*, Archer recalls his time as a "gang-fighter, thief, poolroom lawyer." His experience on the wrong side of the law no doubt made him a good cop in his days on the Long Beach force, as his efforts to help Tom Rica indicate. And his experience on both sides of the law no doubt shaped the humanely intelligent character he exhibits in his role as private investigator.

But one other experience was also crucial to the formation of the mature Lew Archer, his army stint in the Second World War. In *Find a Victim*, the gun battle scene brings back "the smells of cordite and flamethrowers and scorched flesh, the green and bloody springtime of Okinawa." Just as the war was largely responsible for Macdonald's becoming a writer, so has it shaped his detective's consciousness of the extreme manifestation of man's inhumanity to man. And since Archer continually confronts characters whose own psyches were shaped by this global conflict, his experience provides him a base for comprehension of their actions.

We have then in Archer the makings of a man with the perfect sensibilities for a detective. He knows firsthand the complex forces of a modern childhood, rebellious adolescence, and the global madness called war which are the roots of the psychic destruction in the pasts of most of the murderous, conniving characters in the novels.

After the war, Archer put his expertise to work as a policeman with the Long Beach Police Department. That foray lasted only five years before he had to quit because

> There were too many cases where the official version clashed
> with the facts I knew.... Most good policemen have a public
> conscience and a private conscience. I just have a private
> conscience, a poor thing, but my own.

The comment, aside from alluding to Shakespeare, establishes Archer as a man of principle who prefers to operate on his own terms rather than within a system which he knows to be corrupt. It marks him as an idealist, but an idealist grounded in the reality of war, crime, and institutional corruption, a man who prefers to function as an outsider, an outcast, rather than support the system's deceptions. It is this grounding which sets him apart from the doomed, dreamy idealists whom he continually encounters in the novels.

Following his tour as a policeman, Archer installs his private conscience in a small office at 8411½ Sunset Boulevard, a simple place decorated with mug shots. Initially he does mostly divorce work. His business rapidly expands to blackmail, extortion, and missing persons cases, all of which inevitably unravel into murder cases. When we first meet Archer, he is living in a five-room bungalow in a middle-class, residential neighborhood of Los Angeles. It is the same house which he shared with his former wife, Sue, before their divorce, and is a place to which he seldom returns until sleep is overdue. A discussion in *The Barbarous Coast*, which speaks of the second bedroom being used on an on-again, off-again basis and finally turned into a study "which for some reason I hated to use," suggests the poignantly trying demise of his relationship with his wife and, perhaps, the sexual incompatibility at its root. Archer's relationship with women is a persistently difficult problem, which serves to emphasize his own painful loneliness and fallibility and which appears to be finding solace only in his most recent adventure, *The Blue Hammer*.

Archer always gives as the reason for his divorce the fact that Sue did not like his line of work or the hours and company he kept. Such a criticism would be understandable.

When on a case, Archer is likely to go 24 hours or more
without a shave, clean shirt, or break for sleep. His non-
stop, total absorption over the two to four day period which
is typically the time frame for a book makes for suspense
and a powerful, driving narrative, but his style would un-
derstandably make for an unfortunate relationship with a
woman seeking stability and security.

Archer's method of operation is as simple as his life style.
It rarely involves anything more scientific than a contact
mike for listening through walls, or a set of assorted keys
for picking old locks. Only once in the novels, in *The Goodbye
Look*, is a chemical analysis used to confirm a clue and, in
that case, the substance is sent out to a professional labo-
ratory. Archer's primary tools of detection are photographs,
tape recordings and paintings from the past, and his primary technique is waiting and talking, "waiting for truth
to come up to the surface." People spill out their secrets to
him because he is an accomplished questioner, a gifted listener and because "people like to talk about what's hurting
them. It takes the edge off the pain sometimes." This recognition of the commonality of human pain and suffering in
which Archer participates suggests the Dostoevskian vein
which Macdonald works throughout his novels. (See Chapter 6.)

In his description of his Reno colleague, Arnie Walters,
Archer provides us with the requisite "qualities of a first-
rate detective: honesty, imagination, curiosity, and a love
of people." The description applies equally well to Archer
himself. He has a deep-seated sense of honesty which he
violates only rarely and with good cause. He recognizes
most lies instantly and is always left with the taste of bile
when circumstances place him in the position of telling them
himself. His active imagination is responsible for the organizing visions which flash across his mind connecting and
juxtaposing bits of evidence to finally reveal the hidden
pattern, the meaning of a case. His insatiable curiosity leads
him to press his old green Ford convertible up and down the
length of California and across the moutains or to catch a
plane half-way across the country for the purpose of linking

up a dangling lead. And often the trips are at his own expense. His love of people is evident in scenes like the opening of *The Doomsters* where a stranger of unknown mental stability comes knocking on his door, and Archer invites the man into breakfast, commenting, "it was one of those times when you have to decide between your own convenience and the unknown quantity of another man's trouble."

But again, none of this description is meant to suggest that Archer is any more than human or that he is not aware of his own weakness and fallibility. He is criticized in the books and is capable of self-criticism. In *The Moving Target*, Betty Fraley says, "there's something about the way you look at things, wanting them but not liking them. You got cop's eyes—they want to see people hurt." It is a fair critique of the early Archer who takes a more vindictive approach to his work. In *The Doomsters*, Tom Rica, the boy whom Archer tried to help the way he was helped by the old alcoholic detective sergeant, has reverted to his old ways and gives Archer quite a dressing down:

> You want to know why I'm a hype? Because I got bored with double-mouthed bastards like you. You spout the old uplift line, but I never seen a one of you that believed in it for himself. While you're telling other people how to live, you're double-timing your wife and... chasing any dirty nickel you can see.

Remembering the history of their relationship, Archer recognizes that "there was enough truth in what he said to tie my tongue for a minute." In *The Far Side of the Dollar*, Susanna Drew, an old flame, charges that Archer is not really interested in people, but only in the connections between them, "like a plumber."

As Howie Cross pointed out in *Meet Me at the Morgue*, it is difficult to know where one's interest in other people ceases to be humanitarian and becomes an avoidance of self or an attempt to play God. But as early as *The Ivory Grin*, Archer recognizes that "I shouldn't try to master-mind other people's lives. It never works out." More recently, in

*The Blue Hammer*, he has progressed to a finer self-consciousness that allows him to reflect more searchingly. He observes that Fred Johnson

> like other lost and foolish souls, . . . had an urge to help people, to give them psychotherapy even if it wrecked them. When he was probably the one who needed it most. Watch it, I said to myself, or you'll be trying to help Fred in that way. Take a look at your own life, Archer.
> But I preferred not to. My chosen study was other men, hunted men in rented rooms, aging boys clutching at manhood before night fell and they grew suddenly old. If you were a therapist, how could you need therapy? If you were a hunter, you couldn't be hunted. Or could you?

Considering Archer's attempt to enforce salvation on Tom Rica, even if it wrecked him, and his statement in *The Goodbye Look* that "I like to move into people's lives and then move out again," this reflection marks a significant occasion where the probing eye turns inward briefly, recognizes the humanity within, and then turns mercifully away rather than examine too closely the structure of psychic defenses prepared over decades of battles between the selfish and the altruistic. As Eudora Welty observed in her review of *The Underground Man*, Archer has progressed from an early cynicism to a later more human vulnerability.

We cannot expect an extensive analysis of the mental processes and motivations of the detective. By design, he only serves as a catalyst for other people's stories. But Macdonald has provided us with a device for examining the subconscious regions of Archer's mind. We can make such an examination through his dreams and the disembodied visions which he experiences as the result of some of the beatings he takes.

One of Archer's most powerful dream images comes in his first book, *The Moving Target*. He is sitting on a toilet seat in a cheap bar avoiding the deputy sheriff whom he does not want to see. He hasn't eaten for twelve hours. He falls asleep sitting up and his vision is of a long whitewashed corridor slanting down into the bowels of the earth. I followed it down to the underground river of filth that ran under the city.... I had to wade the excremental river.

With the aid of stilts and wrapped in cellophane, he makes it across "untainted." On the other side he "mounted a chrome-plated escalator that gleamed like the jaws of death." It lifts him "through all the zones of evil to a rose-embowered gate" which a gingham-clad maid opens singing *Home Sweet Home*. "It was the central square of the city, but I was alone in it." His footsteps echoed and "the hunch-backed tenements muttered like a forest before a storm." A few pages later, another dream picks up at the same place and we are told "death lurked behind the muttering windows, an old whore with sickness under her paint." The object at the end of the long journey through the filth of the world is still death. And it is inescapably confronted alone. Many of the characters with whom Archer deals are systematically avoiding the contemplation of death, and this denial of their own finitude defines their central weakness. For Archer, too, the subject is a fearful one held at a distance in the subsconscious, but that distance provides him with a perspective from which he can deal with death and seek to resolve its stranglehold on the psyche. Analogously, Archer provides Macdonald with the distance necessary to confront his own psychic terrors while the novels themselves offer their community of readers distance for contemplation of shared fears. In this way, the mystery writer serves as detective hero to the society, providing contemporary parables which allow a detached meditation upon common fears, guilts, and sorrows.

Archer's dreams consistently find him in very isolated places or involve other very isolated, lonely people. They reinforce the alienation which is apparent in his everyday, waking life and no doubt stem from his unattached, disconnected existence. However, not all such images are negative. In *The Barbarous Coast*, Archer dreams of "a man who lived by himself in a landscape of crumbling stones." The man

vaguely remembered some kind of oral tradition to the effect
that a city had stood there once. And a still vaguer tradition:
or perhaps it was a dream inside of the dream: that the people
who had built the city, or their descendants, were coming back
eventually to rebuild it. He wanted to be around when the
work was done.

In *The Underground Man,* a dream envisions the universe
as "one of those boxes of gears that engineers fool around
with." In this vision of unity, he understands "that the ratio
of output to input was one to one." Such visions portray a
complexity of mind that can perceive a hope for future re-
newal or the wisdom of the relationship between effort and
accomplishment, even amidst a world of crime and death.
     Many of Archer's dreams display his typically human
shortcomings. Again in *The Underground Man,* he dreams
that he is "due to arrive someplace in a very short time."
But when he goes outside, he finds "my car. . . had no
wheels, not even a steering wheel. I sat in it like a snail in
a shell and watched the night world go by." In contemporary
dream analysis, cars are often taken to represent the self.
An incomplete car signifies a subconscious recognition of an
incomplete self. What a "complete self" would be is, of
course, a matter of conjecture. Human beings are by nature
incomplete, interdependent pieces of the totality of humanity. The dream suggests that Archer at least knows himself
flawed.
     Archer's most obvious "incompleteness" is his inability to
relate meaningfully to women. The problem may well be one
of form. We should consider Macdonald's statement that
"the main trouble with Archer, and it's also his saving
grace. . . [is that] he doesn't become so involved. . . that he's
used up by a book." Since Archer is a reappearing character,
he can not establish relationships that must be carried from
book to book. The form virtually demands an isolated, singular protagonist; it reflects the alienation of an age and
appeals to the sensibilities of an alienated reader who, perhaps, views him- or herself as an isolated resolver of the
mysteries of the world. There are instances, of course, like

Macdonald's own *The Ferguson Affair*, in which the protagonist is relatively happily married and leads a fairly normal life. Hammett's *The Thin Man* also comes to mind. But
*The Ferguson Affair* is one of Macdonald's least popular
efforts, perhaps for the very reason that it omits Archer,
and although *The Thin Man* contains some brilliant dialogue, it never quite succeeds as a detective story. Its main
character appears almost too bound up with his own social
life and drinking to take the mystery seriously.

But despite the limitations which tend to militate against
the inclusion of meaningful, adult alliances between men
and women, a detective's relationship with women is still a
central feature of the genre. In the works of a writer like
John D. Macdonald, for example, the subject is often treated
in terms of the protagonist, Travis McGee, taking a woman
to bed to make her feel good about herself, saving her from
her own self-pity. Or in the works of a writer like Mickey
Spillane, the male-female relationship exhibits a sado-mas-
ochistic slant bordering on soft pornography.

Macdonald falls victim to neither of these clichéd traps.
Archer's own natural attractions to women and his conscious recognition of the perils of submitting strictly to desire are well illustrated in *The Doomsters*. At one point,
while admiring Mildred Hallman's sleeping face, he catches
himself up short, "recognizing a feeling I'd had before. It
started out as paternal sympathy but rapidly degenerated,
if I let it. And Mildred had a husband." Later, he catches
himself musing that if Mildred's husband failed to survive,
she "would need a man to look after her." For this near
submission to his own lust, he gives himself "a mental kick
in the teeth." In a still later scene, Archer witnesses Sheriff
Ostervelt make a coarse pass at Mildred. The scene stings
his eyes with anger, but

> something held me still and quiet. I'd been wearing my anger
> like blinders, letting it be exploited, and exploiting it for my
> own unacknowledged purposes. I acknowledged now that my
> anger against the sheriff was the expression of a deeper anger
> against myself. In plain terms, he was doing what I wanted to
> be doing.

Such self-analysis is a characteristic of Archer which at once humanizes him and sets him apart from his contemporaries.

Archer's perpetual introspection, however, does not keep him totally celibate. In *The Goodbye Look*, for example, he has a brief affair with Moira Smitheram, but after one night at her house he leaves without waking her and drives away through the morning fog blanketing her cliff-top house. His clandestine departure suggests that he is unwilling to face the consequences of the morning after, while the heavy fog hints at his own mental state that is still unable to relate purposefully to women. In *The Underground Man*, Archer refuses Ellen Storm's offer to share her bed. When she asks, "What are you afraid of, Archer?" he finds it "hard to say," but knows he doesn't want to "commit myself to her until I knew what the consequences would be." Knowing the consequences beforehand is, of course, a difficult, if not impossible task. Archer's relationships with women are still hampered by the complexities of his own past involvements and those of others with whom his work has placed him in contact.

In *The Blue Hammer*, Macdonald achieves his strongest portrait of a contemporary, intelligent, liberated female and through her, Archer, though haltingly, takes the first steps toward resolution of the puzzle of his own romantic needs and fears. Early in the novel, while consoling Paola Grimes, he is still keeping a close eye on himself, thinking, "that the grief you shared with women was most always partly desire." When he meets Betty Jo Siddon, he is aware of "vibrations on the air. . . .[and] in my body" when she leaves the room. He recognizes that he has been "feeling lonely of late" but he also feels "dubious about jumping the generation gap. It could open up like a chasm and swallow you." He is no doubt recalling the numerous cases he has witnessed where an older man's desire for a younger woman has been the cause of a series of disasters.

But after a brief stint of working jointly on the case, Archer finds himself in bed with Betty Jo in what is prob-

ably one of the briefest, most obliquely described love scenes
in all of detective fiction:

> I returned to my motel. Betty Jo came in with me to compare
> notes. We compared not only notes.
>     The night was sweet and short. Dawn slipped in like some-
> thing cool and young and almost forgotten.

Archer and Betty Jo play lovers' games throughout the
book. When he is unable to find her at one point, he leaves
a note which he signs simply "Lew." "Then, after a moment's indecision, I wrote the word 'Love' above my name."
After another moment's hesitation, he

> had a sudden urge to recall it and cross out the word I had
> added. So far as I could remember, I hadn't written the word,
> or spoken it to a woman, in some years. But now it was in my
> mind, like a twinge of pain or hope.

The novels have consistently demonstrated that a lack of
love is one of the basic maladies besetting the modern world.
In this most recent book, Archer begins to recognize that
his own lack of love is a contributing factor in his own
unhappiness. Although there is no clear resolution of his
relationship with Betty Jo in the novel, their liaison does
walk the narrow path between pain and hope to end on a
final positive note. The last scene in which we see Betty Jo
reverses the image of the last night Archer spent with
Moira Smitheram in *The Goodbye Look*. In this instance,
the woman, Betty Jo, leaves before Archer awakes—not
because she can't handle the consequences of their night
together, but because she is involved in the case herself and
has her own story to write. She also leaves out for him food,
milk, a safety razor, and a note which helps resolve the case.
Their relationship is thus redeemed by an equality unlike
any that Archer has previously known; it lacks any of the
qualities of exploitation characteristic of most of the male-
female relationships in the novels and marks a new level of
optimism for both Archer and Macdonald.

But whatever the ultimate resolution of Archer's romantic dilemma, the effect of his long history of love problems
is to mark him as human. His fallibility is an important
theme in Macdonald and is nowhere more evident than in
the overall design of *The Doomsters*. In its final scene
Archer recalls "the day in the past when this story should
have begun for me, but didn't." He remembers a hot day
when he was feeling especially "sweaty and cynical" after
a failed attempt at a reconciliation with his wife, Sue. He
had drunk five or six Gibsons with lunch and was looking
forward to a beach date "with a younger blonde who had
some fairly expensive connections." Tom Rica had interrupted his drunken, self-occupied state with what he realizes now was information which might have allowed him to
prevent the whole string of murders that the book chronicles. But he didn't want the blonde to see him with this
piece of human trash from the streets. He realizes now that
"when Tom stood in my office... I saw myself when I was
a frightened junior-grade hood in Long Beach, kicking the
world in the shins because it wouldn't dance for me. I
brushed him off." He also understands that "it isn't possible
to brush people off, let alone yourself. They wait for you in
time, which is also a closed circuit." *The Doomsters* describes
that closed circuit. In its very first paragraph, Carl Hallman, one of the victims of the last three years of disruption
in the Hallman family, stirs Archer out of a dream. He is
the past catching up. In his final revelation, the image
Archer describes is of the *uruboros*:

> When you looked at the whole picture, there was a certain
> beauty in it, or justice. But I didn't care to look at it for long.
> The circuit of guilty time was too much like a snake with its
> tail in its mouth, consuming itself. If you looked too long,
> there'd be nothing left of it, or you. We were all guilty. We had
> to learn to live with it.

Unlike Chandler's idealized hero, Archer is both tarnished
and afraid, tarnished by universal guilt and afraid of "the
treacherous darkness around us and inside of us." He is

human, life-sized. Macdonald has called him "a democratic
kind of hero," and has spoken of him as "a fairly good
man. . . . [who] embodies values and puts them into action."
These basic values encompass compassion, mercy, and an
undying regard for the young and the underdog. He says as
early as *The Barbarous Coast*, "The problem was to love
people, try to serve them, without wanting anything from
them. I was a long way from solving that one." Leslie Fiedler, in his fine study *Love and Death in the American Novel*,
has suggested that

> the private eye. . . is the cowboy adapted to life on the city
> streets, the embodiment of innocence moving untouched
> through universal guilt.

While such criticism may apply to much "private eye" fiction,
we can see that Archer is a radical departure from that
tradition. And this very achievement of the fallible, tainted,
fearful detective marks one of Macdonald's major contri-
butions to the development of the genre.

But as fascinating a character as Archer is, we must still
recall that he is not the author's primary concern. Rather
he is a vehicle, "a consciousness in which the meaning of
other lives emerges." In Archer, Macdonald has broken with
Chandler and Hammett and the other writers who developed the "new detective" in *Black Mask*. His intention is
"to bring this kind of novel closer to the purpose and range
of the mainstream novel." The purpose of the *Black Mask*
writers, as Chandler once put it, was "to get murder away
from the upper classes, the weekend house party and the
vicar's rose garden, and back to the people who are really
good at it." Macdonald's purpose has been, and remains, to
grapple with and present the most profound human conflicts (evil, death, sexuality, love) "so that the humanity of
all sides is made clear." He achieves that purpose through
what might be called "the style of revelation." Archer consistently functions not to achieve justice according to some
preconceived abstraction but to assist the characters whose
lives he touches in having their own revelations about their

place in the world, their relationship to time, and the avenues of action open to them. And, much as Archer serves as revealer of the truth to the characters of the novels, Macdonald plays the role of revealer to his reading public.

In *The Instant Enemy*, Archer is left alone for a brief period in a room in which a painting by Klee hangs. He has known painters and frequently remarks on paintings in the books. As he is staring at this one, he thinks, "The man was in the maze; the maze was in the man." That image aptly describes both Archer's own life and the intricacy of Macdonald's achievement. Archer is the man in the maze of the mysteries in which the books place him and that maze of a fragmented world is reflected in his own mental processes and psychological development. That complex relationship between inner and outer, between objective and subjective worlds, between other people and self, defines the modern human dilemma and does so within a strictly popular form capable of being read by "all kinds of people." It is a notable accomplishment.

# The Roots of Evil

## Themes and Motifs

You can't speed up time. You have to pick up its beat and let it
support you.
*The Moving Target*

Macdonald has said that the subject of his work, indeed of
all mystery fiction, is evil. But what, exactly, is the nature
and source of the evil in his novels? And how does Macdonald's perception of this evil compare or contrast with the
"mainstream" of modern American fiction? Macdonald is
openly writing about the creation of a new phase of civilization in California, the end of the West. It can be instructive, therefore, to consider briefly both the relationship of
that effort to other conceptions of America itself as such a
creation, and the effect which civilization has historically
been taken to have on human development.

R.W.B. Lewis, in *The American Adam*, sees the American
psyche and therefore American fiction as rooted in the notion of a new start. He perceives the basic flaw in the consciousness of the New World as the idea that a new start
justifies a radical break with the confinements and responsibilities of the Old World. The transition from established
order to virginal wilderness fostered an artificial sense of
freedom, of a world in which the individual no longer needed
to respect the restraints of a rigorously structured society.
Lewis describes the typical American hero as:

... an individual emancipated from history, happily bereft of
ancestry, untouched and undefiled by the usual inheritances
of family and race; an individual standing alone, self-reliant

and self-propelling, ready to confront whatever awaited him with the aid of his own unique and inherent resources.

The implied tension between egoistic freedom and social responsibility is a major theme in American fiction; the selfishness and ignorance of such egocentrism are the primary forces behind many of the crimes in Macdonald's novels. Mark Twain's *Huckleberry Finn* is the classic embodiment of the dream of escape into an idyllic, personal world of social irresponsibility. But even Huck Finn, in the end, is recaptured into the social order, and is fearful that "Aunt Sally she's going to adopt me and sivilize me, and I can't stand it."

That innate fear of civilization, intrinsically masculine (as will be argued later), offers another clue to the source of evil. Historically, it is interesting to note that as late as 1772 Dr. Johnson omitted the word *civilization* from his *Dictionary*. The word *civilize* (forerunner of *civilization*) only came into the English language in the seventeenth century. It came via French from Latin where its basic sense was "to make a criminal matter into a civil matter, and thence, by extension, to bring within a form of social organization." But this increasing social organization (bringing the "criminal" within the institutional structures of the "civil") has frequently been viewed with a skeptical eye. As early as Rousseau, according to Raymond Williams, there existed "a persistent sense of the loss of original human nature through the development of an 'artificial' civilization." Even Coleridge, the subject of Macdonald's doctoral dissertation, wrote of civilization as "a mixed good, if not far more a corrupting influence." That sense of loss, or *alienation*, hinted at by Rousseau and Coleridge is partly attributable to a lingering theological sense of estrangement from the knowledge of God and largely to a shrinking sense of the value of the individual in a highly structured, technological society. In its broader contemporary use, *alienation* has generally taken on the psychological sense of "a loss of connection with one's own feelings and needs."

All these senses of the word *alienation* inform the fiction of Ross Macdonald, from the opening of his first book to the close of his most recent. In the first chapter of *The Dark Tunnel*, we read a description of Detroit that ends: "The men run round in the buildings like apes in iron trees. A new kind of jungle." On the last page of *The Blue Hammer*, we read:

> He peered out at the city we were driving through as though its shadowed streets were alien.
> I felt the strangeness, too. The halls of the courthouse were like catacombs. After an elaborate proceeding that reminded me of the initiation rite into a tribe of aborigines, the D.A.'s men ushered me into the presence of the man I had taken.

Both the modern urban wilderness and its ritualized systems for dealing with aberrant conduct are pictured as cut off from the essentially human.

Presumably there was a time in the not-too-distant past when such alienation was not so urgent a problem. The world of a man's influence was relatively small (the city-state, feudal fiefdom, country manor, village, or small town) and, inversely, his impact upon that world was relatively large. Most individuals were presumably able to identify themselves with a necessary function within their own societies. And the world itself was infinitely large, allowing adequate space between these isolated societies for autonomous development. While we should be careful not to oversentimentalize the physically arduous, often violent societies of classical and medieval times, we do sense that they may have operated on "a more human scale," meaning without the sense of alienation which afflicts the modern world.

But events in modern times have shattered that "human world" forever. Among those shattering events must be reckoned the development of expanded trade, industrialization, the "death of God" (or at least of the classical gods), the mass media, and, most importantly, war on a new scale. Macdonald has analyzed this latter subject:

> As far as the Western world in general was concerned, it was the First World War that permanently altered the moral land-

scape. The first great mass slaughter that occurred in any modern war occurred in the First World War, and it really changed the emotional and spiritual tone of the Western world for keeps. That was a big change, but it didn't really hit us until the Second World War, where we were much more deeply involved. Not just in the amount of human losses, but also in our commitment to this philosophy.

That virtually all of Macdonald's novels involve at least one character involved in and altered by the Second World War cannot be overlooked. Practically all these figures were in their element in the war and never found equal satisfaction in their later lives. Larry Chalmers, in *The Goodbye Look*, is so immersed in the mystique of war that he has perpetrated a hoax over more than two decades about his heroic achievements in a place where he never was. Mark Blackwell, in *The Zebra-Striped Hearse*, has created his own private hell by trying to incorporate military regimentation into the daily disciplining of his daughter.

But what is this fascination? War expresses the essence of alienation. In the contemporary world, alienation is a measure of the diminution of the foreseeable effect of individual action. As the world shrinks into what Marshall McLuhan has called "the global village," individuals come to recognize their own insignificance beside the awesome political, economic, and social forces that rule that world. A common reaction to that realization is a withdrawal into selfishness, a tendency to view the world in terms of Self (Ego) against Other and to treat that Other as expendable.

War objectifies and reinforces these notions. In war, the world is clearly divided into Us and Them and the soldier (usually male) operates within an artificial structure of masculine companionship for the explicit and condoned purpose of obliterating Them, the Other. Many of Macdonald's characters find their finest sense of achievement in that unreal struggle. It fulfills for them Huck Finn's adolescent fantasies of ever greater (masculine) "adventures amongst the Injuns."

And, again recalling Huck Finn, it is not surprising that that same deeply ingrained hostility against a socio-economic-political structure in which one feels insignificant is turned, in time of peace, against women. In a patriarchal society, the most obvious representation of Other is Woman. And like Meyer, the father in *Find a Victim*, who is incapable of comprehending the simple fact that women are human, men create their own tragedies through insensitivity and stupidity. In *Huckleberry Finn*, the first chapter defines the struggle between the masculine and feminine worlds. Huck is continually pressured by the Widow Douglas and her sister to learn spelling, keep his feet off the table, and sit up straight. Women embody the civilizing influence, and, in their commitment to family and the attendant responsibilities, they undermine the masculine urge for freedom and adventure. Or if they recognize their own power over men, like Bess Benning in *The Ivory Grin*, they use it to further their own selfish ends.

Macdonald never suggests that women are completely faultless or that they lack their own sense of alienation. Roughly half his killers are women. But, characteristically, they are the victims of years of psychological oppression at the hands of the patriarchy. Mrs. Snow, in *The Underground Man*, sees her first murder as a blow for justice against the tyrannizing, womanizing Leo Broadhurst. Mildred Hallman's murdering ways, in *The Doomsters*, are the result of the combined pressures of Dr. Grantland and Senator Hallman and the grotesque abortion at the gunpoint of Alicia Hallman, herself a victim of generations of male domination. The primary instance of reversal of this theme comes in *The Chill*. Tish Macready's obsessively possessive love defines the insensitive, consuming evil of that book and she is assisted in her ruse by two other women, her sister and Mrs. Hoffman. But even in this instance, the values expressed (the sense that money can buy happiness) are values imbibed at the knee of a powerful, materialistic father. A portrait of the great patriarch hangs prominently in each sister's residence. Such women are what they are largely as a result of the socializing forces operative in the modern masculine world. Nevertheless, a woman's sense of alienation and isolation may still spark a violent eruption since, as Archer says, "girls can do about anything boys can do when they set their minds to it."

But the alienation which fosters the split between men and women and which finds its clearest expression in war is not limited to violence between the sexes or politically opposed nations. It extends to an alienation from other people, from nature, and finally from the continuum of time and human experience—particularly, in Macdonald's works, an alienation from the past. This latter, especially, would revoke the continuity of history and human development to leave man adrift and a stranger even to himself.

California is a particularly apt setting for demonstrating this modern plight. Archer stands on the beach one evening in *The Drowning Pool* and reflects on man's relationship with nature:

> They had jerrybuilt the beaches from San Diego to the Golden Gate, bulldozed superhighways through the mountains, cut down a thousand years of redwood growth and built an urban wilderness in the desert. They couldn't touch the ocean. They poured their sewage into it but it couldn't be tainted.

After three centuries of trekking across the wilderness of America in search of a new Eden, man has come upon it in California and failed to recognize it. His impulse is to alter it, consume it, pollute it, destroy it. But though nature may be wounded, it will not succumb. The ocean, at least, survives even the black overflow of Man's greed in *Sleeping Beauty*.

But Macdonald's predominant concern is alienation from the past. In *The Three Roads*, he makes an eloquent statement on the modern perception of discontinuity between past, present, and future. Paula West is struck by the contrast between the "ugly huge cube of a building" which houses the San Diego gas company and the "archaic and sentimental incongruity" of the old Santa Fe station across the street.

> It seemed to her that the two buildings were symbols of historic forces. On the one hand was the giant mass of the power

and utility companies that actually dominated the life of the state; on the other, the Spanish past that California plutocracy used to stucco its facade.

The shining metal streamliner waiting beside the station added the final touch to her allegory. It was the impossible future superimposed upon the ugly present in the presence of the regretted past. There was no continuity between the tenses, she thought. You passed from one to the other as a ghost passed through a wall, at the risk of your own reality.

In *Meet Me at the Morgue,* Archer says that Seifel, "was a self-tormented man, living in the past or for the future, always despising the present that could save him." The present is the place where life is lived, but that present cannot exist in isolation from the past out of which it developed. Earlier, in *The Three Roads,* one of the doctors explains that:

Past and present are so intertwined that you can't abandon one without losing your grip on the other. Loss of the present is a fair description of insanity.

And in *The Zebra-Striped Hearse,* Archer recognizes that Pauline Hatchen is feeling pain because she has begun "to realize the consequences of the sealed-off past."

Man exists in a fragile state. His life is perpetually present but inextricably linked to the past and inevitably lived in terms of the future. For the sake of his own sanity, he must come to some kind of terms with those incongruous tenses. But it is a delicate matter and one in which he risks substantial change, as a ghost risks alteration of his ethereal form in passing through a solid wall.

Macdonald's characters respond to this difficult problem in a variety of ways. Anthony Galton, in *The Galton Case,* and other "dreamy idealists" in the novels try to run away from their pasts and fall victim to murder. Nelson Fredericks, in the same book, tried to stop time by disappearing, but the past caught up to him and demanded his life. As Archer realized in *The Doomsters,* time is a closed circuit which can not be simply brushed aside.

But the most persistent manner in which Macdonald's
characters relate to the past is through the Oedipal myth
or father search. It is well to remember that the Oedipal
story is not simply a favorite myth for Macdonald but something he views as "present in every child's life" and which
for him "was almost a case of life imitating myth." Of his
characters, Stanley Broadhurst in *The Underground Man*
pursues the father search with the greatest energy and to
the most ironic end. His obsession destroys his relationship
with his wife and son and ultimately gets him murdered
and buried in the same hole in which his father was in-
terred. His motivation in the search is self-identity, but it
is a search for self-identity which takes as its goal the fixing
of blame on another human being (typically a parent). Such
incentives deny the central truth at the base of all Macdonald's finer stories: the truth of universal guilt. The truth
from which all Macdonald's Californians are fleeing is the
fact of human finitude, i.e. personal death. Bound up with
that denied revelation, is the truth of limitation, of inevitable shortcoming in the face of the possible. Being human
means being unable to act faultlessly; it means being guilty
in a sense not unlike the Biblical notion of original sin.
Archer recognized most clearly in *The Doomsters* that we
are all guilty and must learn to live with it. But guilt is a
difficult problem for Macdonald's characters to grapple
with. Their efforts run to extremes. Some, like Stanley
Broadhurst, deny personal guilt and attempt to find a cul-
prit in the past. Some, like Sampson in *The Moving Target*
or Tappinger in *Black Money*, attempt to use money or sex
or both to deny both the past and their own finitude, thereby
to deny guilt, and to construct a bright, new, artificial world
in the present devoid of the mark of the past, the taint of
guilt, and, hopefully, the truth of death. Or there are those
whose lives are marked by the "futile guilt," described in
*The Three Roads*, whereby characters, generally of the
younger generation (like Bret Taylor in *The Three Roads*,
Carl Hallman in *The Doomsters*, or Dolly Kincaid in *The
Chill*), swing to the opposite extreme and accept the guilt
for actions which they never committed. These unfortu-

nates experience what in *The Chill* is called "the worst
guilt," that of "a child. . . forced, by sheer instinctive self-
preservation, to turn against her parents."

But Macdonald has suggested a solution to this complex
problem and his novels enlighten that possibility. Speaking
about clinical psychology, he has said that "the effect of a
successful analysis is to revalue and in a sense revoke the
past." In Freudian terms, a similar notion is spoken of in
terms of making the unconscious conscious. Macdonald's
most successful novels portray characters who find peace,
if they find it at all, in a revaluation and revocation of the
stranglehold of the past. Harriet Blackwell, for example, in
*The Zebra-Striped Hearse* comes to realize her own complic-
ity in the series of events that have culminated in her
plight: running across borders to escape the consequences
of her own past. The last scene describes her initial step
back toward a guilty, but reconciled, present. In *The Galton
Case*, Anthony Galton/John Brown, Jr.'s physical absence
from the long past acts that culminated in his father's death
would seem to render him guiltless. But even his innocence
is tarnished. He did attempt to murder his murdering stepfather and shares, finally, in responsibility for Fredericks's
suicide. Indeed, his very existence has been responsible for
his mother's last two dreadful decades. In the end, he sees
the vile pattern of which he is a part and vows, hopefully,
not to repeat it. Even Ginny Fablon, in *Black Money*, comes
face to face finally with the reflection of the unreal world
she plotted to create and is able to turn away from it.

All these examples demonstrate new attitudes toward the
past as a result of a recognition of a personal connection
with that past, but perhaps Macdonald's sharpest lesson on
a proper relationship with the past can be inferred from his
choice of pseudonym. His first preference was John Macdonald, his father's name (John Macdonald Millar). When
confusion with John D. MacDonald became a problem, he
substituted the common Canadian name Ross. He thus
chose consciously and deliberately to identify himself with
his own lost father and with the common elements of the
country which shaped his youth. The implication is that we

*are* our fathers and we *are* the circumstances of our rearing. The proper response to this realization is acceptance and continuance: to accept the guilt of the past, but to continue in a new present with a recognition of the freedoms which one does have to affect the here-and-now. In *The Chill*, Alex Kincaid reflects on his relationship with his tyrannical, possessive father. Archer has suggested to him that a total abdication to his father's desires is a kind of self-annulment, self-negation. Alex has realized he was right and says: "It's really amazing, you know? You really can make a decision inside yourself. You can decide to be one thing or the other." Archer reflects quietly: "The only trouble was that you had to make the decision every hour on the hour. But he would have to find that out for himself." Archer's, and Macdonald's, point is that that hourly conscious decision is the essence of responsibility and humanity; it is not easy, but it is the only alternative to a blind, mindless acquiescence to the dark vortex of forces from the past which otherwise consume one's life. It is also that decision to constantly re-assess and re-value one's relationship with all that has gone before which, in a sense, revokes the controlling power of the past by bringing that power to consciousness.

Though Macdonald's characters do frequently achieve a reconciliation with the past, in the limited sense of the familial past, other sources of alienation remain. Alienation in the broader sense of individual estrangement from the world, the Other, is everywhere obvious in the novels. Its presence is proclaimed primarily in descriptions of faces and eyes, the windows of the soul. In *The Blue Hammer*, Archer says of Paola Grimes:

> Her eyes stayed on my face. Through them I could sense the movements of her mind almost as tangibly as if she were playing chess or checkers on a board, asking herself what she had to lose to me in order to take a greater amount away.

This alienation is reflected again in Chantry's paintings which "resembled windows into an alternative world, like the windows that jungle travelers use to watch the animals at night." But whether the description is of actual eyes or the paintings which serve as windows to the artist's soul, the sense is still of a world very private, very personal, very cut-off from the rest of the world, the Other, the rest of humanity.

Throughout his novels, Macdonald consistently utilizes an imagistic device which attempts to indicate both the universality of this division and the possibility of re-forging it into a whole. The imagery employed is that of water and the sea, frequently in connection with a description of a character's eyes. In *The Dark Tunnel*, for example, when Branch first meets Ruth, he says, "I looked for irony in her eyes, which were green and cool as the sea, and saw it flickering deep down near the sea-floor." In *Blue City*, he speaks of "the shifting play of hidden currents" in Mrs. Weather's eyes. In *The Galton Case*, Archer says of Cassie Hildreth, "Our eyes met. Hers were dark ocean blue. Discontent flicked a fin in their depths." The effect of this method of description is to conjure up the classically Freudian image of a limited conscious ego afloat on vast, submerged layers of repressed fears, thoughts, and desires. The correspondence is sharpened at a point in *The Doomsters* when Archer, certain that some of the information he has been given is untrue, says: "The sense of discrepancy persisted in my mind, a gap in the known through which the darkness threatened, like sea behind a dike." The image of a dike separating the known from the threatening darkness evokes the Freudian concept of the "censor" between the conscious and the unconscious. Closer attention to the manner in which ocean/water imagery affects Archer himself is revealing.

In *The Drowning Pool*, the detective says "the smell of the sea. . . flooded my consciousness like an ancestral memory." In *The Chill*, he speaks of "the sea. . . surging among the pilings like the blithe mindless forces of dissolution." Although Archer is a good swimmer, he says in *The Moving Target:*

I stood for a minute in the zone of wet brown sand just above the reach of the waves and looked at them. The waves were blue and sparkling, curved as gracefully as women, but I was afraid of them. The sea was cold and dangerous. It held dead men.

In *The Wycherly Woman,* Archer describes his dreams as he is falling asleep:

the old movie projector I was using for a brain wouldn't shut down. It kept on grinding out aquatic scenes in which I became immersed, sinking like a spent swimmer in coiling cold water, through deepening zones of chill where the dead thronged like memories, their lank hair drifting in the underwater currents.

Consistently, these submersion images are linked with fear, death, dissolution. They express the terror experienced by an individual, isolated consciousness in contemplation of its own finite end.

But Macdonald also asserts that these vast depths can be navigated. Having spoken of Archer as "a transitional figure between a world that is breaking up and one coming into being in which relationships and people will be important," Macdonald embodies his strongest statement of the possibilities of that new world in Archer's relationship with Betty Jo Siddon in *The Blue Hammer.* After Archer's first night with her, he is sitting by the window in a dockside restaurant having breakfast, watching the boats, and thinking: "They [the boats] gave me the emphatic feeling that I was in motion, too, scudding along under complex pressures and even more complex controls toward the open sea." The pressures and controls of external forces are recognized to be complex, but he has been released toward the open sea. This freedom is not the egocentric freedom at the root of evil. Rather, it is the freedom or release experienced by the selfish ego when it is finally able to comprehend its connection with other human beings and to come to a greater awareness of both its commonness and limitations. It is the release that portends the bridging of the inner self with the external reality of the Other.

Much in the way that the single image of the boat sailing toward the open sea frames the idea of release through connection with others, namely Betty Jo, all of Macdonald's water imagery fits a thematic pattern. The effect of using similar imagery for both the external world and the private world behind the eyes is to collapse the internal and external, the subjective and the objective within a single figure. The revelation suggested is that external truth is reflected in internal truth and vice versa. Archer's understanding of these connections is furthered in *The Blue Hammer* through still another natural image. The leader of the strange religious sect that has taken over the old Chantry house confronts him by saying:

> You seem to be a man engaged in an endless battle, an endless search. Has it ever occurred to you that the search may be for yourself? And that the way to find yourself is to be still and silent, silent and still?

Archer ponders the questions a moment and then concedes privately: "Perhaps, after all, the truth I was looking for couldn't be found in the world. You had to go up on a mountain and wait for it, or find it in yourself." The yoking of the internal search with the mountain further develops the idea of the objective collapsed within the subjective and subjective projected onto the objective and recalls the man-in-the-maze/maze-in-the-man image from *The Instant Enemy* (see Chapter 5). Man is thus by these figurative devices restored to a position as a part of the whole of creation; the resolution of the human dilemma in Macdonald is far from complete, but the gulf of alienation is at least imagistically bridged.

This essay began by implying a connection between alienation and evil. It has outlined how alienation of the individual from nature, from other human beings, and from himself are all aspects of modernity and of the fiction of Ross Macdonald. Perhaps it has still not been specific enough about that word *evil*. Quite simply, egoism, the sense of disconnected, individual freedom, is the source of evil. Evil, so defined, manifests itself in selfishness, greed, and ignorance. When the self is profoundly disconnected by such hubris, the separation violates the sense of community and the actions of the self no longer benefit human kind. Crime is antisocial behavior which is a product of hubris and which is systematically strengthened by the increasingly alienating forces within society. One of the earliest and most respected chroniclers of this phenomenon was Macdonald's acknowledged mentor, Dostoevsky. One of Dostoevsky's central themes is the doubleness of the individual. It is a doubleness which reflects a world comprising life and death, creation and destruction, good and evil, body and intellect. Dostoevsky maintains, according to Temira Pachmuss,

> that man, in view of these antitheses in God's creation, tends to regard himself as a transitory creature, as insignificant and meaningless as any other phenomenon on earth. This fills him with despair.

His characters, in flight from this despair, typically run to the extremes of expressing either a power-oriented, rational self (like Raskolnikov in *Crime and Punishment*), or a petty, spiteful self (like the narrator of *Notes from Underground*). Macdonald himself has spoken of a similar doubleness, "an unstable balance between reason and more primitive human qualities," as a "characteristic of the detective story" and sees the genre as dealing with "the nightmare [that] can't quite be explained away and persists in the teeth of reason." The nightmares that motivate both Dostoevsky's and Macdonald's characters have common roots and the two author's resolutions of them also demonstrate resemblances.

R. P. Blackmur, in his essay on *Crime and Punishment*, has summarized the Dostoevskian resolution by pointing out that for him:

> the edge of the abyss of sin was the horizon of salvation by faith, and suffering was the condition of vision. Sin was the Crime, and the suffering created by faith was the Punishment.
> If we push the operation of this insight one step further, it becomes evident that the act of life itself is the Crime, and

that to submit, by faith, to the suffering of life at the expense
of the act is to achieve salvation—or, if you like a less theological phrase, it is to achieve integration or wholeness of
personality

For Dostoevsky, crime is the nature of life. Salvation is
achieved through suffering. The concept is not far from the
Christian idea of atonement for original sin. And parallels
can be readily drawn in the works of Ross Macdonald.

In *Find a Victim*, Hilda Meyer is informed of the affair
being carried on by her husband, Brandon Church, and her
sister, Anne. The confirmation of this relationship which
she had suspected and feared releases a pent-up emotional
flood that distorts and confuses external reality with her
own inner turmoil. She hears the church bells ringing for
early Mass and takes the bells as a sign. The bells continue
to ring in her ears as she drives to the lake cabin and don't
stop until the gun goes off and her sister is dead. Her dis-
tortion of reality reaches such an extreme that she "thought
for a minute that it was me, lying dead on the floor. I ran
away." In the final scene, she confuses her husband with
her father and is ripping up the plants in the garden with
her bare hands because "they're not pretty any more." And
the last we see of her she is

back among the flowers, ripping the last of them out of the
moist earth. . . . The planter was denuded and she had begun
to strip the thorny lemon tree. Church washed and bandaged
her bleeding hands before they took her away.

The scene is richly symbolic. First, all the elements of alienation are presented: from nature (ripping up the flowers),
from other people (confusing her father and husband), and
from herself (thinking—perhaps wishing—that her sister's
dead body were her own). Moreover, traditional religious
symbols underscore the action. The church bells, thorny
tree, bleeding hands, and her husband's name (Church) all
serve to suggest a parallel with the Christ story. Concerning
his intentions in this passage, Macdonald has said that:

suffering people are naturally and of necessity the object of religious feelings. When anyone is suffering psychologically, I feel that relationship [with traditional religious images] is worth mentioning—to show that suffering is not limited to great religious figures.

As for Dostoevsky, Macdonald's concern is for the suffering necessitated by the crimes which are a condition of life. Frequently in Macdonald, that suffering is mitigated through suicide (as Dostoevsky once considered ending *Crime and Punishment*). But in his finer works, Macdonald demonstrates the redeeming qualities of suffering. In *Find a Victim*, for example, the fact that Church (literally her husband, figuratively the institution) is binding her bleeding hands suggests a possible resolution of Hilda's private suffering in the hands of a sympathetic community.

A strong statement of the redemptive powers of suffering comes in *The Blue Hammer*. William Mead has spent twenty-five years atoning for his personal crimes. His private suffering is emblemized by a pietá in which he included a self-portrait as the suffering Christ. When his ordeal is ended in the final scene, he is "pale and weak and worried," but his natural father, from whom he has been estranged all his life, steps forward to restore the continuity of family and history. He has not had to expend his life, like Stanley Broadhurst, in a futile search for a past which he can blame. Rather, his suffering has expiated his guilt and opened the way for a recognition of his real identity and a restoration to community.

The actions of other characters, like Harriet Blackwell in *The Zebra-Striped Hearse*, also reflect this recognition of a need for a return to community through suffering and expiation of the personal guilt which is a product of egoism. And even Stanley Broadhurst—though he does not survive—in his double burial and "resurrection" symbolizes the suffering which life exacts as retribution for the selfish sins of the human race.

Macdonald's model for action in this world of sin and crime and inhumanity is Archer himself. A guilty, isolated, lonely figure, he has suffered from his own inability to bridle his ego in relations with other human beings (primarily women) and from the psychological scars of his own modern childhood and adolescence. As he grows older and more aware, he realizes that:

> The hot breath of vengeance was growing cold in my nostrils. . . . I had more concern for a kind of economy in life that would help to preserve the things that were worth preserving. No doubt Leo Broadhurst had been worth preserving—any man, or any woman was—

And his sense of economy in life extends to balancing out his own guilt for murdering Puddler in *The Moving Target* by bringing in Rico alive in *The Blue Hammer* after a fight scene closely parallel to the fight with Puddler more than twenty years earlier. "Rico," he says, "whatever his sins, had served as an equalizer for one of mine."

Macdonald was quoted in Chapter 1 on the necessity of discovering a way to express values in this technological age where they are not present in the society. The chief value in the Macdonald world view proves synonymous with the Socratic dictum, "Know thyself." Evil, whether in Plato's world or Archer's, arises from ignorance, specifically ignorance of and/or a refusal to accept the truth of personal mortality. The great obstacle to conquering this ignorance is the apparent paradox of a finite mind and body trapped within the infinite, circular sweep of time. The problem for the individual is to find an appropriate relationship between his or her finite existence and the infinity of the whole, to find some reconciliation of the incongruous tenses. Such revelation can not happen instantaneously. It is a process of struggle for insight into one's human origins and relationships and that insight is finally manifested in a release from the egoistic drives for power and dominance, an acceptance of one's parents as only human, and a recognition of the futility of self-pity.

The "sorrow of finitude" is a phrase particularly expressive of the human dilemma portrayed in Macdonald's novels. Though the phrase originated in the philosophy of Hegel, it is also applicable to Martin Heidegger's interpretation of human existence and by extension to Macdonald. According to Heidegger, the German existentialist, the sorrow is a consequence of the finitude. Because humans are finite, we can never know the totality of meaning. Each action, each choice in the face of multiple possibilities forever closes off the possibilities not chosen. What might life have been like for Stanley Broadhurst if his father had not chosen to have an affair with Marty Nickerson? Or what might it have been like for Harriet Blackwell if her father had not chosen to try to rear her in his own image? Such questions have no fruitful answers. Those possibilities are forever concealed. That much is concealed is the nature of human existence; it is the nature of authenticity and wisdom, according to Heidegger, to accept what is concealed as concealed and to allow what *can* be disclosed to *be* disclosed. This is likewise the wisdom of Ross Macdonald. His instrument for conveying this insight is his "democratic hero," Lew Archer. Archer is a figure of compassion—compassion developed through his own struggles with his own egoism— who steps into other people's lives for the purpose of revealing the truth, whatever it may be; let the chips fall where they may. When his mission is accomplished, he departs to allow the affected persons to make their own adaptation to the truth so revealed.

# A Delicate Tension

## Macdonald's Style

> I felt that I was getting closer. . . and I moved from picture to picture looking for his style or his signature.
> *The Zebra-Striped Hearse*

Essentially, style refers to an author's manner—*how* he says what he says rather than *what* he says or *why* he says it. Literary analyses of style tend to concentrate on such elements as diction, or choice of words; sentence structure and syntax; use of figurative language, like similes and metaphors; and characteristic patterns of rhythm and sound. A comparative analysis of the styles of crime fiction writers might include such other elements as manner of description, attention to plot, and characterization.

Eudora Welty has said of Ross Macdonald's style that it

> is one of delicacy and tension, very tightly made, with a spring in it. It doesn't allow a static sentence or one without pertinence. . . . It is an almost unbroken series of sparkling pictures.

The central figurative device in Macdonald's style, the one used most often to convey those "sparkling pictures," is the simile—similes which Welty has called "beautiful and audacious."

Perhaps the most persuasive argument for the unique appeal of Macdonald's similes can be made through a close inspection of their use in one novel to support and clarify the author's general themes. *The Underground Man* offers many opportunities for such evaluation.

On the occasion of his first visit to the gardener, Fritz

Snow, in his cell-like room, Archer is struck by the thin beams of sunlight seeping through the drawn blind.

> They were thrust across the room *like the swords of a magician probing a basket to demonstrate that his partner had disappeared.* As if he would like to disappear indeed, the gardener crouched in the corner of the iron bed with his feet pulled up under him. . . . He peered at the swords of light thrust through the chinks in the blind *as if they were in fact the probes of a rational universe finding him out.* [Italics of similes are mine throughout.]

The figure draws both a literal picture of the observable appearance of the room and a psychological portrait of the unobservable mental processes of its occupant. Literally, Fritz Snow lives in a dark box which tries, unsuccessfully, to deny the reality of the outside world, but that reality slips quietly, accusingly in at every chink and crevice. Figuratively, Fritz has withdrawn into the dark, private quarters of his own mind and seeks desperately to avoid any confrontation with the threatening external world. Macdonald's effort to portray alienation is closely sustained by his choice of figurative language; *what* he has to say becomes intimately linked to *how* he says it.

Another telling use of simile comes when Archer is confronting Brian Kilpatrick—father of the boy who has disappeared on his neighbor's boat, manager of suspect real estate deals, ex-husband of one of the women involved with Leo Broadhurst years before, and current lover of an over-the-hill, bikini-clad sot. When he walks to the bar for a drink, Archer says he moved *"like a caged animal that had paced out the short distance many times."* When Archer challenges him to break out of his self-pity and act to save the missing youngsters, Archer says, "I caught a glimpse of the broken seriousness which lived in him *like a spoiled priest in hiding."* Later he speaks of Kilpatrick *"moving like something mechanical and pre-aimed."* This juxtaposition of seemingly disparate images demonstrates Macdonald's ability to evoke ambiguous responses from the reader toward a character. Macdonald, especially in his later fiction, is not interested in drawing black-and-white characters. His intention is to describe believable human beings in response to overwhelming, but credible circumstances. In *The Doomsters* Archer dreamed of himself as a caged animal and we can believe that he harbors some sympathy for another man similarly trapped. But when Kilpatrick shows no signs of acting within the options open to him, Archer lashes out at him and then conjures the "broken seriousness. . . spoiled priest" image. That figure suggests a former seriousness shattered by some previous attempt at action in the world and now withdrawn from confrontation in the way that a priest, spoiled (in the sense of "ruined") by the rebuff of an overly idealistic approach to the world, might turn his idealism inward as protection. The image has both positive and negative aspects: positive in the suggestion that an earlier attempt at action was made, negative in that withdrawal was the reaction to failure. And even though Kilpatrick is obviously a despicable character in his real estate dealings, the comparison of his movements to "something mechanical and pre-aimed" tempers our criticism of him by its suggestion of his comparative ineffectuality in the face of the larger forces which have molded his life.

Within such a world view of overwhelming, divisive forces, the simile is a particularly apt device; it can both underscore the fragmentation that obscures correspondence and suggest the re-forging of unities. The characterizations of Fritz Snow and Brian Kilpatrick imply the divisions; Nature provides the images of wholeness. Midway through *The Underground Man*, at a point where Archer has knocked himself out on the case with little result and dreamed of his own ineffectuality, the jays awake him demanding peanuts. As he scatters the nuts over the lawn and the jays swoop to gather them, he says, "It was *like watching a flashing blue explosion-in-reverse that put the morning world together again.*" The unity is in nature, in a holistic perspective larger than the individual, and, though simile is appropriate, it is surely not the only method for demonstrating such truth. Plot serves a similar function in Macdonald.

The plot of *The Zebra-Striped Hearse* may be taken as

characteristic in this respect. Archer's investigation is nec-
essarily restrained at each stage by the limited facts avail-
able to him. He first must confirm or deny the guilt of Bruce
Campion. Having convinced himself on that point, he must
find another suspect. Circumstances suggest that Isobel
Blackwell is a likely candidate. When she is cleared of connection with the murders, suspicion turns to Mark Blackwell and finally to Harriet. Throughout this shifting focus,
the reader is carried along by the detective and is privy to
all the information he acquires. Nothing is ever sprung on
the reader at the climax in the style of a Sherlock Holmes
or of a book like Hammett's *The Thin Man*. It is a credit to
Macdonald's mastery of the form that he can lay all the
facts before his reader and still have his detective achieve
a dramatic resolution through his excellent memory, refined
sense of human nature and extended awareness of the connectedness of people and events. Macdonald has criticized
Chandler for describing a good plot "as one that made for
good scenes, as if the parts were greater than the whole"
and has defined his own position in these terms:

> I see plot as a vehicle of meaning. It should be as complex as
> contemporary life, but balanced enough to say true things
> about it. The surprise with which a detective novel concludes
> should set up tragic vibrations which run backward through
> the entire structure. Which means that the structure must be
> single, and *intended*.

Macdonald's plots are singular, intended, and tragic. In *The
Zebra-Striped Hearse*, once we have understood the complexities of Mark Blackwell's concerned, if misguided, fa-
therly affections; the passions behind the hostility of Harriet Blackwell; the pawn-like role played by Isobel
Blackwell; and the simultaneously involved and detached
idealism motivating Bruce Campion; we can appreciate the
single thread of despair that holds all these lives together.
And we can see each of them playing out their roles *in
character* from the very first page of the book. But we do
not see this unity until the end on a first reading. The

immediate task is always interpreting the objective actions
of characters as they occur. Is Bruce Campion a gold-digger
or an idealist? Is Harriet Blackwell running from something
done to her or something she has done herself? The reader
is wise not to leap to any conclusions before the end. But
once that end is achieved, the singular, tragic story of the
Blackwell family reverberates back through the book to the
very first scene where Mark Blackwell is described as looking *"like a man being rotated by invisible torque."*

A virtually faultless use of simile and a startling virtu-
osity for plot complication are the most striking elements
of Macdonald's style, but they are not the only aspects of
his writing that render him unique. He has also polished
the art of dialogue to a luster seldom rivalled. It is not un-
common to open one of the later books to any chapter at ran-
dom and find the entire chapter written in dialogue with
only the rarest intrusion of an explanatory paragraph or
Archer's reflections. Even the identifying tag "he said" or
its stand-in is rare. And, in much the same way that Macdonald's style progresses to a greater reliance on dialogue,
it also clearly shifts from an early, heavily expository manner to more cinematic representations.

A comparison of two similar scenes from an early and a
later work illustrate the point. In *The Three Roads*, Bret
Taylor gets very drunk and has a vision of death and the
ultimate futility of life. In *The Blue Hammer*, a similar vision comes to Mildred Mead. The narrative treatment of the
two scenes is markedly different. Bret Taylor's vision is
described in this manner. (It should be recalled that *The
Three Roads* is Macdonald's only use of third person nar-
ration.)

> For the second time that day he felt the black wind blowing
> him toward extinction and the grave, futureless and untor-
> mented by even the first pricks of consciousness, merged care-
> lessly with the filth and trash of generations, without a his-
> tory or a thought to disturb the long serenity of blankness,
> the timeless gestation of the final dust. Because he wished
> himself dead he ordered and drank a double Scotch, and an-

other, and another. They gave him back his desire to live, but turned his inward loathing outward.

Mildred Mead experiences a similar self-loathing and takes her own step to the edge of self-destruction. Archer describes it this way:

> I looked up at the four-sided clock on the courthouse tower. It was ten. There was only one person visible on the observation platform, a white-headed woman whose rather clumsy movements caught my eye. Mildred. She paused and turned and gripped the black iron fence. It was almost up to her chin. She peered over it, down into the stone-paved courtyard.
>
> She was extraordinarily still. She looked like a woman staring down into her grave. The life of the city seemed to freeze in widening circles around her. . . .
>
> When I stepped out on the observation platform, she had turned to face me, her back against the iron fence. She turned again and tried to clamber over the fence into empty space. Her lame old body failed in the attempt.
>
> I put my arms around her and held her securely. She was breathing as if she had climbed the tower hand over hand. The frozen life of the city resumed, and I began to hear its sounds again.
>
> She struggled in my arms. 'Let me go. . . . I'm the hag of the universe.'

In the earlier scene, the representation is strictly verbal and interior. In the later one, the state of mind is rendered through images which are external to the character but which elucidate her mental condition. They are images which would be readily translatable to film and which invite the reader to make his own interpolations. The style of *The Three Roads* provides a totally self-sufficient explanation of the event. The style of *The Blue Hammer* provides the images which allow the reader to evaluate and come to his own conclusions. The clock tower and its chin-high black fence suggest the irrevocable trap of time. The city freezing as in a still movie frame evokes Archer's total absorption in the predicament of this other human being. Mildred's own feeble strugglings underscore the reality of her despair. The

two scenes articulate a similar emotion, but with Mildred
Mead the method of its portrayal is of a higher order. The
achievement of a literary statement through external symbol is a more complex and demanding form than the interior
musings and ravings of an individual character. And it is
such an achievement on the grander scale of the fire in *The
Underground Man* or the oil spill in *Sleeping Beauty* which
distinguishes Macdonald from his contemporaries.

Other aspects of the author's style which should be considered are his descriptions and characterizations. Many of
Macdonald's fine characterizations of central figures in the
works have already been pointed out in the discussions of
individual novels. The salient feature of these characterizations is typically their brief but engaging precision and
the subtle manner in which they focus and clarify the
broader concerns of the novels. A particularly noteworthy
bit of such characterization appears in *The Blue Hammer*.
Archer arrives at Francine Chantry's party and is introduced to the other guests by Betty Siddon:

> She introduced me to Colonel Aspinwall, an elderly man with
> an English accent, an English suit, and a young English wife
> who looked me over and found me socially undesirable. To Dr.
> Ian Innes, a cigar-chomping thick-jowled man, whose surgical
> eyes seemed to be examining me for symptoms. To Mrs. Innes,
> who was pale and tense and fluttering, like a patient. To Jer-
> emy Rader, the artist, tall and hairy and jovial in the last late
> flush of his youth. To Molly Rader, a statuesque brunette of
> about thirty-nine. . . . And to Arthur Planter, an art collector
> so well known that I had heard of him.

Within a few words, each character is brought crisply to
mind and the general tenor of the gathering is established.
There is internal consistency as well. The doctor has "sur-
gical eyes" and a wife who flutters "like a patient." The
artist's wife is "statuesque." And beneath it all is Archer's
self-deflating wit which calls attention to the gathering's
elitism: the art collector is so well known that even *he* has
heard of him. The passage reflects a well-turned craftsman-
ship.

Macdonald is equally adept at brief descriptions of scenes
and events which serve his thematic purposes. In *The
Doomsters* he finds himself at a drive-in hot dog stand and
describes this scene:

> A boy and girl in a hand-painted lavender Chevrolet coupé
> made me feel better, for some reason. They were sitting close,
> like a body with two ducktailed heads, taking alternate sips of
> malted milk from the same straw, germ-free with love. Near
> them in a rusty Hudson a man in a workshirt, his dark and
> hefty wife, three or four children whose eyes were brilliant
> and bleary with drive-in-movie memories, were eating mus-
> tard dripping hot dogs with the rapt solemnity of communi-
> cants.

Within a paragraph, a concise image of contemporary American culture is drawn. Adolescent love finds bliss in a shared
malted milk; the working class family finds its relief from
the mundane world in drive-in movies and hot dogs. There
is simultaneously hope and criticism in the description. The
endless discovery of juvenile love makes Archer feel better
while the vision of the family eating "with the rapt solem-
nity of communicants," we may surmise, hints at the culture's total secularization. The hot dog stand becomes the
altar of the modern world's materialism; value lies in con-
sumption. Such deft mixing and interplay of thematic con-
tent within a very short space is characteristic of Macdonald's particular narrative ability.

There are also lesser stylistic idiosyncrasies that distinguish Macdonald. One of the most intriguing is his diction
or choice of words. The great majority of the vocabulary in
the novels is the common language of everyday life. Macdonald has obviously made an attempt to keep his vocabulary current through the inclusion of such youth-culture
phrases as *freaked out, uppers* and *downers,* and *going
around with my mind in a sling.* But one also comes frequently across such words as: *detritus, cenotaph, defalca-
tions, dudgeon, rictus, spoor, caracul,* and *wimple.* A walk
may lead to a *pergola;* a face may be low-browed and *prog-
nathous;* feet descending stairs may be heard as soft *susur-*

*rus;* or a pianist may strike a *plangent* discord. Two explanations for this occasional incursion into inflated diction seem possible. One is that Macdonald's erudition is such that he does not recognize when he is straining the verbal limits of the average reader. The other, and more likely, is that, given his stated desires to "reach and educate" and to "write books that can be read by all kinds of people," such words function as "teasers" to the less wise to improve their vocabularies and as shibboleths to the enlightened.

Another significant element of Macdonald's style is his use of humor—as a means of humanizing Archer and placing him on the side of the underdog, as a relief from the psychological or physical violence of the narrative, or as a means of structuring relationships between characters. The latter case is illustrated by an incident on the first page of *The Galton Case.* Archer arrives at Sable's office and, ignored by the receptionist, he finds "a Harvard chair [that] stood casually in one corner. I sat down on it, in the interests of self-improvement, and picked up a fresh copy of the *Wall Street Journal.*" When he is finally noticed and told that Sable is not in, he remarks: "I got up out of the Harvard chair. It was like being expelled." Macdonald has called attention to this wry bit of self-mockery as "structure on a small scale." It suggests in a brief scene all the material, educational, and social differences between Sable and Archer. And for those with an awareness of Macdonald's life, the joke has a private side—he was once refused a graduate fellowship at Harvard.

The self-deflating nature of Archer's wit is also evident in a later incident in the same novel. In a rare scene of violence, Archer has been beaten to unconsciousness, recovered enough to lash out anew at his attackers and been beaten again into submission. As he recovers from the last assault, he thinks:

> It was a bad afternoon. Quite suddenly it was a bad evening. Somebody had awakened me with his snoring. I listened to the snoring for a while. It stopped when I held my breath and started again when I let my breath out. For a long time I missed the significance of this.

There is both humor and pathos in such a passage: humor in the ironic manner of its telling and pathos in the realization that a man of Archer's sensibilities should be reduced to such mismatched physical battles with hoodlums.

But Archer's dry humor is at its best when provoked by incompetence, frequently the incompetence of small-time law officers with big-time pretensions. Early in *The Galton Case*, Archer gets lost, as he often does in the hilltop mazes which meander among the homes of his wealthy clientele. In the course of his wandering, he comes upon a wrecked car and decides to check it for clues. Two sheriff's deputies arrive and one holds a gun on him while the other frisks him:

> He was very thorough. He even investigated the fuzz in my pockets. I commented on this.
> "This is no joke. What's your name?"
> ... I was angry and sweating. I opened my mouth and put both feet in, all the way up to the knee.
> "I'm Captain Nemo," I said. "I just came ashore from a hostile submarine. Curiously enough, we fuel our subs with seaweed. The hull itself is formed from highly compressed seaweed. So take me to your wisest man. There is no time to be lost."

The passage serves both to illuminate Archer's character and to place him clearly on the side of the underdog. Though he frequently cooperates with the authorities, his own police experience makes him particularly critical of police methods. When he confronts an inexperienced or incompetent law officer, his reaction is typically one of not-so-subtle derision. Though he obviously could not make such remarks if he were not secure in his own role, they reflect sympathy for all the Tom Ricas and Carl Hallmans of the world who never see any other face of the law.

Welty called Macdonald's style "one of delicacy and tension, very tightly made." Even the accuracy of this description does not obviate its perhaps necessary vagueness. Nevertheless, we can finally suggest that there at least a few concrete, indisputable things to be said about Ross Macdonald's style. It relies heavily upon simile for the yoking of images which frequently sustain the author's themes. Virtually every sentence contributes to the movement of the author's incomparably complex plots. As the novels develop, they depend more heavily upon simple sentences, uninterrupted dialogue, and scenes of cinematic quality. Characterization is economical and precise, reflecting insight and careful observation of human nature. Diction runs the gamut from the colloquial to the flamboyant. Wit, finely wrought, draws attention to the ironies and absurdities of the world. In short, Ross Macdonald has crafted a style superbly suited to his chosen genre and a model for his successors.

# A California Mythology

## Macdonald's Achievement

> There was more to it than that.
> There always is.
> *The Doomsters*

Any effort to place Macdonald's literary achievement—whether within the restricted field of detective novelists or the broader spectrum of modern fiction—should first attempt to separate criticism of the genre from criticism of Macdonald as practitioner of that genre. One of the few literary critics of stature to take the genre seriously and to direct his attention to Macdonald specifically is Geoffrey Hartman. Professor Hartman makes some interesting observations, which can serve as a point of departure. He says:

> to solve a crime in detective stories means to give it an exact location: to pinpoint not merely the murderer and his motives but also the very place, the room, the ingenious or brutal circumstance. We want not only proof but, like Othello, ocular proof. . . .
> . . . sophisticated art is closer to being an antimystery rather than a mystery. It limits, even while expressing, this passion for ocular proof.

Hartman sees the detective story as clearly preferring "the horror of the visible . . . to what is unknown or invisible," suggesting finally that the genre is incapable of dealing with the subtler shadings of psychology and circumstance. While he admits that there are, of course, differences among the styles of American mystery writers and says, for example, that "Macdonald's characters . . . are more credible than Chandler's, because they are more ordinary," Hartman presses on to another significant criticism. In his opinion, the genre avoids moral issues in favor of an "exploitative element" that plays upon a popular desire to believe "that one just man (the detective) will succeed" even though reality, for Hartman, suggests this is not the case. He draws particular attention to *The Goodbye Look* and finds fault with that part of the plot which has Nick Chalmers, at the age of eight, shooting his estranged father, Eldon Swain. He interprets Swain's performance and motivations as "only an act of sentiment and boozy affection" and concludes that "grim mistakes of this kind belong to folklore or high tragedy."

It must be noted, first of all, that such criticism implies several misreadings of Macdonald. To suggest that Eldon Swain's actions in *The Goodbye Look*, for example, are purely the result of "sentiment and boozy affection" is to disregard all the evidence amassed in the plot concerning Swain's *possible* motivations (blackmail, kidnapping, child molesting) and the chronicle of Swain's spiralling moral decline (from banker, to embezzler, to purchaser of another man's daughter). And to speak of Archer in terms of exploiting the reader's gullible desire to believe in perfect heroes is to overlook Macdonald's careful and explicit avoidance of the Chandlerian hero ("neither tarnished nor afraid") in favor of a character as capable of selfishness and failure as any human. In Hartman's final summation, he remarks, perhaps more to the point, that:

> ... the trouble with the detective novel is not that it is moral but that it is moralistic; not that it is popular but that it is stylized; not that it lacks realism but that it picks up the latest realism [Freudianism in Macdonald's case] and exploits it.

As Thomas Edwards, in his review of *The Blue Hammer*, has warned, "It's hard for sophisticated people to like something simple without overrating it." The caution is a good one. But that is not to say that we must accept Hartman's characterization of all detective novels as moralistic, stylized, exploitative, and, by implication, worthless. While his criticisms apply with more force to some detective novelists than others (perhaps more to Spillane than to Hammett, for instance), they make very little room for the unique achievements which are possible in the genre and which Macdonald frequently exemplifies.

It is only fair to agree that there are some rather stringent limitations enforced by the format of the detective story. It does demand a rather pat ending, a conclusion from which "sophisticated art" clearly steers away. The reader does demand to know how all the clues fit together, to see the instrument and circumstance of the crime described (Hartman's "ocular proof"), and to see some semblance of justice achieved. There is also an inherent limitation in the form of the story imposed by a single detective-protagonist who must put together clues by interrogation and whose own past, personality and motivations remain somewhat mysterious. But to call Macdonald's use of Freudian psychology, for example, "exploitation" is certainly to expose a bias against popularizers. Macdonald himself has recognized that

> the writer of popular literature generally doesn't invent too much. He deals with received forms which are familiar to his audience. . . . He deals with . . . second generation ideas. He's generally a little ahead of his audience, but not light years ahead.

If we accept Macdonald's notion that "a community tends to communicate with itself through its fiction," and if we find Macdonald's use of Freudian concepts consistent throughout the novels and with the Freudian tradition, then it becomes difficult to comprehend this as exploitation, certainly in the sense of "unethical."

Similarly, "moralistic" hardly seems a proper term to apply to Macdonald's work. Unquestionably, the novels simplify the evil in Archer's world to a primary concern for sex and money. But as manifestations of the egocentrism at the heart of contemporary American culture and its problems, the tracing of the society's preoccupation with sex and money allows a forum for critiquing that egocentrism. The final result is inevitably gothic terror, but, as Leslie Fiedler has pointed out, "the American novel is pre-eminently a novel of terror." And Fiedler states further that "the final horrors, as modern society has come to realize, are neither gods nor demons, but intimate aspects of our minds." The statement is clearly applicable to Macdonald's basic themes of psychological double-ness and the irrational. But, while Fiedler finds this continual reliance of American fiction on gothic modes a deplorable state, Macdonald would sharply disagree. He believes that:

> the gothic tradition gradually developed into the most all-encompassing literary tradition that we have. The basic reason, I think, is that the world changed in the direction of the gothic so that the gothic became a more and more feasible explanation of it. And I mean by that quite explicitly that the world of fear and violence which existed in Anne Radcliffe's imagination and the world of utter loneliness that existed in the imagination of Coleridge ... have gradually emerged as dominant realities in the modern world and the use of the tradition is inevitable because it's talking about the things that we know and want to understand.

Thus, Macdonald is solidly within a tradition which has consistently explored the subtle, irrational terrors beneath the placid facade of modern civilization and the modern mind. If he has done so within a popular genre, he has committed the act with a conscious, didactic purpose, fully embodying that purpose fictionally, without succumbing to exploitation or mere preachiness.

It may be instructive at this point to reflect upon Hartman's further criticism of detective fiction that "when all is finished, nothing is rereadable." This assertion is rooted in his belief that detective stories lack the dramatic irony characteristic of great tragedy. The multiple layers of meaning which an author is able to suggest by his use of irony are often used as a measure of the author's stature. As M. H. Abrams notes:

> recourse to irony by an author carries an implicit compliment to the intelligence of the reader, who is associated with the

author and the knowing minority who are not taken in by the
ostensible meaning.

The *dramatic irony*, to which Hartman alludes, is defined
by Abrams as irony which

> involves a situation in a play or a narrative in which the
> audience shares with the author knowledge of which a char-
> acter is ignorant: the character acts in a way grossly inappro-
> priate to the actual circumstance, or expects the opposite of
> what fate holds in store, or says something that anticipates
> the actual outcome, but not at all in the way that he means
> it.

The classic example of dramatic irony occurs in Sophocles'
*Oedipus* where the king engages in a hunt for the evil-doer
who has brought a plague upon Thebes and the object of
the hunt proves to be the king himself.

The point of all this is that it is possible to argue the
existence of a kind of dramatic irony in Macdonald's work,
that this irony is only apparent upon re-reading, and that
the re-reading makes the author's ability and his message
shine in a new light. Dramatic irony in Greek tragedy was
effective because the plots were based on legends whose
outcome was already known to the audience. With detective
stories, we must read through once for the outcome and
then re-read to appreciate the author's ironic hand. To give
just one example: when we have read *The Zebra-Striped
Hearse* and know that Harriet is the real murderer, that
Mark Blackwell's psyche was largely shaped by the tyranny
of his own mother, that he has fathered a child by Dolly,
and that he finally commits suicide in an attempt to absolve
himself of his guilt in the whole affair, then we begin to look
very differently on Mark and his bungling belligerence, and
on such early statements as: "You don't know the pressures
I live under. The combined forces of the females in my life—"

This system of irony and re-reading for the fuller texture
of the stories also argues well for Macdonald's own concept
of his work as an attempt to turn Freud's myth-made-psy-

chology back into psychology-made-myth. Abrams defines
*mythology*, in the classical sense, as:

> a system of hereditary stories which were once believed to be
> true by a particular cultural group, and which served to ex-
> plain (in terms of the intentions and actions of supernatural
> beings) why the world is as it is and things happen as they do,
> and to establish the rationale for social customs and obser-
> vances and the sanctions for the rules by which men conduct
> their lives.

In this light, Macdonald's efforts might be seen as a kind of
anti-mythology or mythology on its head. There are no su-
pernatural beings in these stories, but they do attempt to
show "why the world is as it is and things happen as they
do" and they do so by demonstrating a *lack* of rationale, a
*lack* of social customs and observances, and a *lack* of "sanc-
tions for the rules by which men conduct their lives." Macdonald's mythology is the negative mythology of individual
avarice and desire. It is a world without communal value
where man is systematically consuming himself and rav-
aging nature.

All these perspectives might be proposed. Somerset
Maugham once predicted that future literary historians
would "pass somewhat lightly over the compositions of the
'serious' novelists and turn their attention to the immense
and varied achievements of the detective writers." But it
might also be argued that detective stories are simply "es-
capist fiction" and that matters should be left at that. So
great a critic as Edmund Wilson once wrote that the "reading of detective stories . . . for silliness and minor harmful-
ness, ranks somewhere between crossword puzzles and
smoking." The split in opinions on the subject is wide and
not likely to be bridged easily.

The debate will, no doubt, continue. Meanwhile, Macdonald, a highly literate, socially involved man schooled in the
historical development of both fiction and psychology, continues with calm assurance his mission of writing novels
"that can be read by all kinds of people." And if indeed the

purpose of psychoanalysis is "to make the unconscious conscious" (as Freud has put it), then it might be argued that Macdonald is constructing a series of stories that help us to *see* the *evil*, to "feel where the knife is cutting."

As the novels are absorbed into the reader's consciousness, they leave there a personal, residual mythology of characters and plots on the edge of man's technological advance westward that serve the very contemporary purpose of explaining "why the world is as it is and things happen the way they do," that help us become conscious of the evil within our collective unconscious—a mythology of the mass mind, of contemporary society.

Finally, the novels reflect not only a cultural mythology but also, as with all great fiction, the record of the author's own personal struggles to comprehend the world and his own place in it. As Macdonald has described the writing process:

> The character holding the pen has to wrestle and conspire with the one taking shape on paper, extracting a vision of the self from internal darkness—a self dying into fiction as it comes to birth.

The struggle of the self for identity, whose record Macdonald has left for us in the pages of his novels, offers a brilliant, vivid image of contemporary consciousness in conflict with itself and surely justifies William Goldman's calling these "the finest series of detective novels ever written by an American." Perhaps in time, when our views of contemporary fiction are less myopic, even some of the restricting qualifiers to greatness in that phrase will fade away.

# BIBLIOGRAPHY

## I. Works by Macdonald

### A. NOVELS

*The Dark Tunnel.* 1944; rpt. New York: Bantam, 1972. Originally published under the name Kenneth Millar.

*Trouble Follows Me.* 1946; rpt. New York: Bantam, 1972. Originally published under the name Kenneth Millar.

*Blue City.* 1947; rpt. New York: Bantam, 1974. Originally published under the name Kenneth Millar.

*The Three Roads.* 1948; rpt. New York: Bantam, 1974. Originally published under the name Kenneth Millar.

*The Moving Target.* 1949; rpt. New York: Bantam, 1970. Originally published under the name John Macdonald.

*The Drowning Pool.* 1950; rpt. New York: Bantam, 1970. Originally published under the name John Ross Macdonald.

*The Way Some People Die.* 1951; rpt. New York: Bantam, 1971. Originally published under the name John Ross Macdonald.

*The Ivory Grin.* 1952; rpt. New York: Bantam, 1971. Originally published under the name John Ross Macdonald.

*Meet Me at the Morgue.* 1953; rpt. New York: Bantam, 1972. Originally published under the name John Ross Macdonald.

*Find a Victim.* 1954; rpt. New York: Bantam, 1972. Originally published under the name John Ross Macdonald.

*The Barbarous Coast.* 1956; rpt. New York: Bantam, 1957.

*The Doomsters.* 1958; rpt. New York: Bantam, 1959.

*The Galton Case.* 1959; rpt. New York: Bantam, 1960.

*The Ferguson Affair.* 1960; rpt. New York: Bantam, 1971.

*The Wycherly Woman.* 1961; rpt. New York: Bantam, 1963.

*The Zebra-Striped Hearse.* 1962; rpt. New York: Bantam, 1964.

*The Chill.* 1964; rpt. New York: Bantam, 1965.

*The Far Side of the Dollar.* 1965; rpt. New York: Bantam, 1966.

*Black Money.* New York: Knopf, 1966.

*The Instant Enemy.* 1968; rpt. New York: Bantam, 1969.

*The Goodbye Look.* 1969; rpt. New York: Bantam, 1970.

*The Underground Man.* 1971; rpt. New York: Bantam, 1972.
*Sleeping Beauty.* 1973; rpt. New York: Bantam, 1974.
*The Blue Hammer.* New York: Knopf, 1976.

## B.   OTHER WORKS BY MILLAR/MACDONALD*

*Archer at Large.* New York: Knopf, 1970. An omnibus reprint of *The Galton Case, The Chill,* and *Black Money* with a Foreword by the author.

*Archer in Hollywood.* New York: Knopf, 1967. An omnibus reprint of *The Moving Target, The Way Some People Die,* and *The Barbarous Coast* with a Foreword by the author.

"A Death Road for the Condor." *Sports Illustrated,* XX, 6 April 1964.

"Life with the Blob." *Sports Illustrated,* XXX, 21 April 1969.

*The Name Is Archer.* 1955; rpt. New York: Bantam, 1971. Originally published under the name John Ross Macdonald. Contents: "Find the Woman," "Gone Girl," "The Bearded Lady," "The Suicide," "Guilt-Edged Blonde," "The Sinister Habit," and "Wild Goose Chase."

*On Crime Writing.* Santa Barbara, Cal.: Capra Press, 1973. Contains the essays "The Writer as Detective Hero" and "Writing *The Galton Case.*"

"A Preface to *The Galton Case.*" In *Afterwords: Novelists on Their Novels,* edited by Thomas McCormack. New York: Harper and Row, 1969.

"The Sleeping Dog." *Argosy,* CCCLX, April 1965.

"The Writer's Sense of Place." *South Dakota Review,* XIII, 3 (Autumn 1975).

[Macdonald] and Robert Easton. "Santa Barbarans cite an 11th Commandment: 'Thou Shalt Not Abuse the Earth.'" *The New York Times Magazine,* 12 October 1969.

[Millar, Kenneth.] "Introduction." To *Kenneth Millar/Ross Macdonald: A Checklist,* compiled by Matthew J. Bruccoli. Detroit: Gale Research Co., 1971.

[Millar, Kenneth.] "The Inward Eye: A Revaluation of Coleridge's Psychological Criticism." Unpublished doctoral dissertation, University of Michigan, 1951.

[Millar, Ken.] "The South Sea Soup Co." In *The Grumbler.* Kitchener, Ontario: Kitchener-Waterloo Collegiate and Vocational School, 1931. Macdonald's first published story.

---

* All written under name of Ross Macdonald, unless otherwise noted.

[Millar, Kenneth and Arthur Kaye.] *Ross Macdonald: "In the First Person."* Time-Life, 1970. A film.

## *II. Works about Macdonald*

### A. MAJOR REVIEWS, LISTED CHRONOLOGICALLY

*The Wycherly Woman*
Robbins, Frank E. Review of *The Wycherly Woman*, by Ross Macdonald. *Michigan Quarterly Review* 1 (Winter 1962): 74.

*The Zebra-Striped Hearse*
Rice, Warner G. Review of *The Zebra-Striped Hearse*, by Ross Macdonald. *Michigan Quarterly Review* 2 (Summer 1963): 212.
Sale, Roger. Review of *The Zebra-Striped Hearse*, by Ross Macdonald. *Hudson Review* 16 (Spring 1963): 141–9.

*Black Money*
Boucher, Anthony. Review of *Black Money*, by Ross Macdonald. *The New York Times Book Review*, 9 January 1966.
Sale, Roger. Review of *Black Money*, by Ross Macdonald. *Hudson Review* 19 (Spring 1966): 124–34.

*The Instant Enemy*
Adler, Dick. Review of *The Instant Enemy*, by Ross Macdonald. *Book World*, 25 February 1968.
Boucher, Anthony. Review of *The Instant Enemy*, by Ross Macdonald. *The New York Times Book Review*, 3 March 1968.
Lask, Thomas. Review of *The Instant Enemy*, by Ross Macdonald. *New York Times*, 6 July 1968.

*The Goodbye Look*
Goldman, William. "The Finest Series of Detective Novels Ever Written by an American," review of *The Goodbye Look* by Ross Macdonald. *New York Times Book Review*, 1 June 1969.

*The Underground Man*
Clemons, Walter. "Ross Macdonald at His Best," review of *The Underground Man*, by Ross Macdonald. *New York Times*, 19 February 1971.
Lingeman, Richard. "The Underground Bye-bye: Still Another Lew Archibald Novel by Ross Macdonald," review of *The Underground Man*, by Ross Macdonald. *New York Times Book Review*, 6 June 1971.
Nordell, Roderick. Review of *The Underground Man*, by Ross Macdonald. *Christian Science Monitor*, 4 March 1971.

Schickel, Richard. "Detective Story," review of *The Underground Man*, by Ross Macdonald. *Commentary*, September 1971.

Welty, Eudora. "The Stuff That Nightmares Are Made Of," review of *The Underground Man*, by Ross Macdonald. *New York Times Book Review*, 14 February 1971.

*Sleeping Beauty*

White, Jean. "Going for the Freudian Vein," review of *Sleeping Beauty*, by Ross Macdonald. *Book World—The Washington Post*, 20 May 1973.

Woods, Crawford. Review of *Sleeping Beauty*, by Ross Macdonald. *The New York Times Book Review*, 20 May 1973.

*The Blue Hammer*

Edwards, Thomas R. "Tough Guys," review of *The Blue Hammer*, by Ross Macdonald. *The New York Review of Books*, 30 September 1976.

Wood, Michael. Review of *The Blue Hammer*, by Ross Macdonald. *The New York Times Book Review*, 12 June 1976.

B.   ESSAYS, INTERVIEWS, AND OTHER WORKS

Abrahams, Etta Claire. "Visions and Values in the Action Detective Novel: A Study of the Works of Raymond Chandler, Kenneth Millar, and John D. MacDonald." Unpublished doctoral dissertation, Michigan State University, 1973.

Bruccoli, Matthew J., comp. *Kenneth Millar/Ross Macdonald: A Checklist*. Detroit: Gale Research Co., 1971. Includes extensive bibliographical information on Macdonald's early sketches and stories, a complete list of reviews written by Macdonald for the *San Francisco Chronicle*, and enumerates all editions and printings of the novels through 1971.

Carroll, Jon. "Ross Macdonald in Raw California," *Esquire*, June 1972. (Based on an interview with Macdonald.

Cook, Bruce. "Ross Macdonald: The Prince in the Poorhouse." *Catholic World*, October 1971.

Crider, Allen Billy. "The Private-Eye Hero: A Study of the Novels of Dashiell Hammett, Raymond Chandler, and Ross Macdonald." Unpublished doctoral dissertation, The University of Texas at Austin, 1972.

Grogg, Sam, Jr. "Ross Macdonald: At the Edge." *Journal of Popular Culture* VII (Summer 1973). Based on an interview with Macdonald.

Holtan, Judith, and I. Orley. "The Time-Space Dimension in the

Lew Archer Detective Novels." *North Dakota Quarterly* (Autumn 1972): 30–41.

Leonard, John. "Ross Macdonald: His Lew Archer and Other Secret Selves." *New York Times Book Review*, 1 June 1967. Based on an interview with Macdonald.

Moore, Richard O. "Ross Macdonald." In *The Writer in America*. New York: Educational Broadcasting Corp., 1977. One of the series of films on *The Writer in America* produced by WNET, New York.

Sokolov, Raymond A. "The Art of Murder." *Newsweek*, 22 March 1971. Based on an interview with Macdonald.

Wolfe, Peter. *Dreamers Who Live Their Dreams: The World of Ross Macdonald's Novels*. Bowling Green, Ohio: Bowling Green Univ. Popular Press, 1976. First book-length study of Macdonald. Includes exhaustive plot summaries of all novels through *Sleeping Beauty*.

## III.  Other works cited

Abrams, M. H. *A Glossary of Literary Terms*. 3rd ed., New York: Holt, Rinehart and Winston, 1971.

Blackmur, R. P. "*Crime and Punishment*: A Study of Dostoevsky's Novel." In *Modern Literary Criticism: An Anthology*, edited by Irving Howe. Boston, Beacon Press, 1958.

Chandler, Raymond. "The Simple Art of Murder: An Essay." In *The Simple Art of Murder*. 1939; rpt. New York: Ballantine Books, 1972.

Fiedler, Leslie A. *Love and Death in the American Novel*. 2nd ed., New York: Dell Publishing Co., 1966.

Hartmann, Geoffrey H. *The Fate of Reading and Other Essays*. Chicago: Univ. of Chicago Press, 1975.

Lewis, R. W. B. *The American Adam: Innocence, Tragedy, and Tradition in the Nineteenth Century*. Chicago: Univ. of Chicago Press, 1955.

Pachmuss, Temira. *F. M. Dostoevsky: Dualism and Synthesis of the Human Soul*. Carbondale, Ill.: Southern Illinois Univ. Press, 1963.

Twain, Mark. *The Adventures of Huckleberry Finn*. 1884; rpt. New York: Washington Square Press, 1960.

Williams, Raymond. *Keywords: A Vocabulary of Culture and Society*. New York: Oxford Univ. Press, 1976.

# Notes

| PAGE | QUOTE | SOURCE |
|------|-------|--------|

bottom of 4–5   all quotes — Millar, *Checklist*.

5   "by other means" — Ross Macdonald, "Foreword" to *Archer in Hollywood* (New York: Knopf, 1967), pp. vii–ix.

6   "of angry rapture" — Millar, *Checklist*, p. xiv.

6   "out of it" — Macdonald, *Archer in Hollywood*, p. vii.

6   "the radioactive material" — Ibid.

7   "dropped the John" — Raymond A. Sokolov, "The Art of Murder," *Newsweek*, March 22, 1971, pp. 101–108.

7   "theory of poetic" — Kenneth Millar, "The Inward Eye: A Revaluation of Coleridge's Psychological Criticism" (Unpublished doctoral dissertation, Univ. of Michigan, 1951), p. 2.

7   "all his disciples" — Telephone interview.

7   "forever ambivalent" — John Leonard, "Ross Macdonald, His Lew Archer and Other Secret Selves," *New York Times Book Review*, June 1, 1967, pp. 2ff.

7   "own small way" — Sokolov, p. 108.

7 after extract–8   all quotes

7   "on my life" — Telephone interview.

7   "Dante to Kafka" — Ibid.

8   "ever met with" — Ibid.

8   "reference to Dostoevsky" — Ibid.

8   "of our lives" — Ross Macdonald, "The Writer as Detective Hero," in *On Crime Writing*, pp. 9–24.

8   "a romantic presence" — Millar, *Checklist*, p. xvi.

8   "the speaking voice" — Kenneth Millar and Arthur Kaye, *Ross Macdonald "In the First Person,"* (Time-Life, 1970), pp. 8–9.

9   "city as inferno" — Macdonald, "The Writer as Detective Hero," p. 13.

9   "in my life" — Sokolov, p. 108.

10   "for the spill" — Ross Macdonald and Robert Easton, "Santa Barbarans cite an 11th Commandment: 'Thou Shalt Not Abuse the Earth,' " *The New York Times Magazine*, 12 October 1969, pp. 32ff.

| PAGE | QUOTE | SOURCE |
|------|-------|--------|
| 10 | "which there is" | Sokolov, p. 108. |
| 10 | "and humanize it" | Ibid. |
| 10 | "you go along" | Jon Carroll, "Ross Macdonald in Raw California," *Esquire*, June, 1972, pp. 148ff. |
| 11 | "around the form" | Ibid., p. 149. |
| 11 | "it with him" | Richard O. Moore, "Ross Macdonald," *The Writer in America* (New York: Educational Broadcasting Corp., 1977), p. 3. |
| 11 | "all kinds of people" | Carroll, p. 149. |
| 11 | "foot in Canada" | Ross Macdonald, "The Writer's Sense of Place," *South Dakota Review*, XIII, 3 (Autumn 1975), pp. 128–35. |
| 12 | "north after all" | Ibid., p. 131. |

## Chapter Two

| PAGE | QUOTE | SOURCE |
|------|-------|--------|
| 14 | "with bells on" | Ross Macdonald, *The Dark Tunnel* (1944; rpt. New York: Bantam, 1972), p. 223. |
| 15 | "empty, echoing pile" | Millar, *Checklist*, p. xiii. |
| 15 | "kind of jungle" | *The Dark Tunnel*, p. 8. |
| 15 | "were effective weapons" | Ibid., p. 21. |
| 15 | "on weak men" | Ibid., p. 244. |
| 16 | "track of themselves" | Ross Macdonald, *Trouble Follows Me* (1946; rpt. New York: Bantam, 1972), pp. 19–20. |
| 18-20 | all quotes | Ross Macdonald, *Blue City* (1947; rpt. New York: Bantam, 1974). |
| 22 | all quotes | Ross Macdonald, *The Three Roads* (1948; rpt. New York: Bantam, 1974). |
| 23 | "in circular motion" | Macdonald, "Writing *The Galton Case*," p. 45. |
| 24 | all quotes | *The Three Roads*. |
| 25, 26, 27 through extract | all quotes | Ross Macdonald, *The Moving Target* (1949; rpt. New York: Bantam, 1970). |
| 27 | "only half alive" | Ibid., p. 182. |
| 27 | "their other values" | Ibid. |
| 27 | "a wrong friend" | Ibid., p. 82. |

| PAGE | QUOTE | SOURCE |
|---|---|---|
| second half of 27–29 | all quotes | Ross Macdonald, *The Drowning Pool* (1950; rpt. New York: Bantam, 1970). |
| 30–32 end of section | all quotes | Ross Macdonald, *The Way Some People Die* (1951; rpt. New York: Bantam, 1971). |
| 32–34 end of section | all quotes | Ross Macdonald, *The Ivory Grin* (1952; rpt. New York: Bantam, 1971). |
| 34–35 | all quotes | Ross Macdonald, *Meet Me at the Morgue* (1953; rpt. New York: Bantam, 1972). |
| 36 | "extracts" | Ross Macdonald, *Find a Victim* (1954; rpt. New York: Bantam, 1972). |
| 37 | "into his voice" | Ross Macdonald, *The Barbarous Coast* (1956; rpt. New York: Bantam, 1957), p. 92. |
| 37 | "in the book" | *Archer in Hollywood*, p. ix. |

*Chapter 3*

| 41–46 | all quotes | Ross Macdonald, *The Doomsters* (1958; rpt. New York: Bantam, 1959). |
| 47 | "sorrows of life" | Macdonald, "The Writer as Detective Hero," p. 21. |
| 47 | all other quotes | Macdonald, "Writing *The Galton Case*." |
| 48–52 to extract | all quotes | Ross Macdonald, *The Galton Case* (1959; rpt. New York: Bantam, 1960). |
| 52–54 | all quotes | Macdonald, "Writing *The Galton Case*," p. 45. |
| 55 | "reality for himself" | Ross Macdonald, *The Ferguson Affair* (1960; rpt. New York: Bantam, 1971), p. 162. |
| 55 | "clogged and contrived" | Peter Wolfe, *Dreamers Who Live Their Dreams: The World of Ross Macdonald's Novels* (Bowling Green, Ohio: Bowling Green Univ. Popular Press, 1976), p. 203. |

| PAGE | QUOTE | SOURCE |
|------|-------|--------|
| 56-57 | all quotes | *The Ferguson Affair.* |
| 58-59 | all quotes | Ross Macdonald, *The Wycherly Woman* (1961; rpt. New York: Bantam, 1963). |
| 60-62 | all quotes | Ross Macdonald, *The Zebra-Striped Hearse* (1962; rpt. New York: Bantam, 1964). |
| 62 | "an astonishing conincidence" | Bruce Cook, "Ross Macdonald: The Prince in the Poorhouse," *Catholic World*, October 1971, pp. 27-30. |
| 63-66 | all quotes | *The Zebra-Striped Hearse.* |
| 67-78 | all quotes | Ross Macdonald, *The Chill* (1964; rpt. New York: Bantam, 1965). |
| 79 | "of inherited wealth" | Ross Macdonald, *The Far Side of the Dollar* (1965; rpt. New York: Bantam, 1966), p. 215. |
| 79 | "anyone at all" | *Ibid.* |

## Chapter 4

| | | |
|------|-------|--------|
| 82-85 | all quotes | Ross Macdonald, *Black Money* (New York: Knopf, 1966). |
| 86 | "awesome as creation" | Ross Macdonald, *The Instant Enemy* (1968; rpt. New York: Bantam, 1969), p. 1. |
| 87 | "cases, foolish virgins" | Ibid., p. 201. |
| 87 | "by an American" | William Goldman, "The Finest Series of Detective Novels Ever Written by an American," *New York Times Book Review*, 1 June 1969, p. 1. |
| 88-95 end of section | all quotes | Ross Macdonald, *The Goodbye Look* (1969; rpt. New York: Bantam, 1970). |
| 95 | "we live with" | Eudora Welty, "The Stuff Nightmares Are Made Of," *New York Times Book Review*, 14 February 1971, p. 1ff. |
| 95-102 end of section | all quotes | Ross Macdonald, *The Underground Man* (1971; rpt. New York: Bantam, 1972). |

| PAGE | QUOTE | SOURCE |
|---|---|---|
| 102-103 | all quotes | Ross Macdonald, *Sleeping Beauty* (1973; rpt. New York: Bantam, 1974). |
| 103 | "Peter Wolfe suggests" | Peter Wolfe, *Dreamers Who Live Their Dreams: The World of Ross Macdonald's Novels* (Bowling Green, Ohio: Univ. Popular Press, 1976), p. 337. |
| 104-108 | all quotes | Ross Macdonald, *The Blue Hammer* (New York: Knopf, 1976). |

## Chapter 5

| | | |
|---|---|---|
| 109 | "he almost disappears" | Macdonald, "Writing *The Galton Case*," p. 41. |
| 109 | "the locked door" | Macdonald, "The Writer as Detective Hero," p. 23. |
| 109 | "of the natives" | Macdonald, *Archer in Hollywood*, p. viii. |
| 110 | "for any world" | Raymond Chandler, "The Simple Art of Murder: An Essay," in *The Simple Art of Murder* (1939; rpt. New York: Ballantine Books, 1972), pp. 1-22. |
| 110 | "and bad guys" | Macdonald, "The Writer as Detective Hero," p. 17. |
| 110 | "other ingenious devices" | *The Doomsters*, p. 21. |
| 110 | "good or ill" | *The Barbarous Coast*, p. 53. |
| 111 | "She always whispered" | *The Chill*, p. 80. |
| 111 | "to no decision" | *The Drowning Pool*, p. 26. |
| 111 | "in the family" | Ibid. |
| 111 | "stubborn mulish terror" | *Find a Victim*, p. 167. |
| 112 | "detective sergeant, me" | Ibid., p. 168. |
| 112 | "thief, poolroom lawyer" | *The Doomsters*, p. 176. |
| 112 | "springtime of Okinawa" | *Find a Victim*, p. 151. |
| 113 | "but my own" | *The Drowning Pool*, p. 139. |
| 113 | "hated to use" | *The Barbarous Coast*, p. 44. |
| 114 | "to the surface" | *The Doomsters*, p. 134. |
| 114 | "the pain sometimes" | *The Goodbye Look*, p. 17. |
| 114 | "love of people" | *The Zebra-Striped Hearse*, p. 97. |
| 115 | "another man's trouble" | *The Doomsters*, p. 2. |
| 115 | "see people hurt" | *The Moving Target*, p. 56. |
| 115 | "you can see" | *The Doomsters*, p. 92. |

| PAGE | QUOTE | SOURCE |
|---|---|---|
| 115 | "for a minute" | Ibid. |
| 115 | "never works out" | *The Ivory Grin*, p. 227. |
| 116 | "Or could you?" | *The Blue Hammer*, p. 98-99. |
| 116 | "move out again" | *The Goodbye Look*, p. 96. |
| 116 | "more human vulnerability" | Eudora Welty, "*The Stuff Nightmares Are Made Of*," New York *Times Book Review*, 14 February 1971, p. 29. |
| 117 | "the excremental river" | *The Moving Target*, p. 109. |
| 117 | "before a storm" | Ibid. |
| 117 | "under her paint" | Ibid., p. 119. |
| 118 | "work was done" | *The Barbarous Coast*, p. 134. |
| 118 | "one to one" | *The Underground Man*, p. 72. |
| 118 | "world go by" | Ibid., p. 108. |
| 118 | "by a book" | Richard O. Moore, "Ross Macdonald," *The Writer in America*, p. 7. |
| 119 | all quotes | *The Doomsters*. |
| 120 | "consequences would be" | *The Underground Man*, p. 207. |
| 120-21 | all quotes | *The Blue Hammer*. |
| 122 | all quotes | *The Doomsters*, p. 176. |
| 123 | "kind of hero" | Richard O. Moore, *The Writer in America*, p. 7. |
| 123 | "them into action" | Ibid. |
| 123 | "solving that one" | *The Barbarous Coast*, p. 87. |
| 123 | "through universal guilt" | Leslie A. Fiedler, *Love and Death in the American Novel* (2nd ed.; New York: Dell Publishing Co., 1966), p. 506. |
| 123 | "other lives emerge" | Macdonald, "The Writer as Detective Hero," p. 24. |
| 123 | "the mainstream novel" | Ibid. |
| 123 | "good at it" | Quoted by Macdonald, "The Writer as Detective Hero," p. 15. |
| 123 | "is made clear" | Author's telephone interview with Millar, Santa Barbara, Cal., 18 April 1978. |
| 124 | "in the man" | *The Instant Enemy*, p. 139. |

## Chapter 6

| 126 | "and inherent resources" | R. W. B. Lewis, *The American Adam: Innocence, Tragedy and Tradition in the Nineteenth Cen-* |

174                                          Ross Macdonald

| PAGE | QUOTE | SOURCE |
|------|-------|--------|
| | | *tury* (Chicago: Univ. of Chicago Press, 1955), p. 5. |
| 126 | "can't stand it" | Mark Twain, *The Adventures of Huckleberry Finn* (1884; rpt. New York: Washington Square Press, 1960), p. 374. |
| 126 | "of social organization" | Raymond Williams, *Keywords: A Vocabulary of Culture and Society* (New York: Oxford Univ. Press, 1976), p. 48. |
| 126 | "an 'artificial' civilization" | Ibid., p. 30. |
| 126 | "a corrupting influence" | S. T. Coleridge, *On the Constitution of Church and State.* As quoted by Williams, pp. 49–50. |
| 127 | "feelings and needs" | Williams, *Keywords*, p. 32. |
| 127 | "kind of jungle" | *The Dark Tunnel*, p. 8. |
| 127 | "I had taken" | *The Blue Hammer*, p. 218. |
| 128 | "to this philosophy" | *Gallery* magazine, Vol. IV, Number 3, March 1976, pp. 84–90. |
| 128 | "amongst the Injuns" | Twain, *Huckleberry Finn*, p. 373. |
| 130 | "minds to it" | *The Underground Man*, p. 40. |
| 130 | "couldn't be tainted" | *The Drowning Pool*, p. 21. |
| 131 | "your own reality" | *The Three Roads*, p. 19. |
| 131 | "could save him" | *Meet Me at the Morgue*, p. 163. |
| 131 | "description of insanity" | *The Three Roads*, p. 10. |
| 131 | "the sealed-off past" | *The Zebra-Striped Hearse*, p. 173. |
| 132 | "life imitating myth" | Raymond A. Sokolov, "The Art of Murder," p. 108. |
| 133 | "against her parents" | *The Chill*, p. 69. |
| 133 | "revoke the past" | Macdonald, *Checklist*, p. xi. |
| 134 | "out for himself" | *The Chill*, p. 114. |
| 134 | "greater amount away" | *The Blue Hammer*, p. 48. |
| 135 | "animals at night" | Ibid., p. 11. |
| 135 | "near the sea-floor" | *The Dark Tunnel*, p. 20. |
| 135 | "Mrs. Weather's eyes" | *Blue City*, p. 34. |
| 135 | "in their depths" | *The Galton Case*, p. 19. |
| 135 | "behind a dike" | *The Doomsters*, p. 119. |
| 135 | "an ancestral memory" | *The Drowning Pool*, pp. 163–64. |
| 135 | "forces of dissolution" | *The Chill*, p. 39. |
| 136 | "held dead men" | *The Moving Target*, p. 134. |
| 136 | "the underwater currents" | *The Wycherly Woman*, p. 212. |
| 136 | "will be important" | Sokolov, "The Art of Murder," p. 108. |
| 136 | "the open sea" | *The Blue Hammer*, p. 67. |
| 137 | both quotes | Ibid. |

| PAGE | QUOTE | SOURCE |
|------|-------|--------|
| 138 | "him with despair" | Temira Pachmuss, *F. M. Dostoevsky: Dualism and Synthesis of the Human Soul* (Carbondale: Southern Illinois Univ. Press, 1963), p. xiv. |
| 138 | "teeth of reason" | Macdonald, "The Writer as Detective Hero," p. 11. |
| 139 | "wholeness of personality" | R. P. Blackmur, "*Crime and Punishment*: A Study of Dostoevsky's Novel," in *Modern Literary Criticism: An Anthology*, ed. Irving Howe (Boston: Beacon Press, 1958), pp. 219–38. |
| 139 | "I ran away" and subsequent quotes | *Find a Victim*. |
| 140 | "great religious figures" | Author's telephone interview with Millar, Santa Barbara, Cal., 18 April 1978. |
| 140 | "weak and worried" | *The Blue Hammer*, p. 218. |
| 141 | "any woman was" | *The Underground Man*, p. 230. |
| 141 | "one of mine" | *The Blue Hammer*, p. 142. |

## Chapter 7

| | | |
|------|-------|--------|
| 143 | all quotes | Eudora Welty, "The Stuff That Nightmares Are Made Of," p. 30. |
| 144–145 | all quotes | *The Underground Man*, pp. 48–49. |
| 146 | both quotes | Macdonald, "The Writer as Detective Hero," p. 22. |
| 147 | "*by invisible torque*" | *The Zebra-Striped Hearse*, p. 6. |
| 148 | "inward loathing outward" | *The Three Roads*, p. 99. |
| 148 | "of the universe" | *The Blue Hammer*, pp. 212–13. |
| 149 | "heard of him" | Ibid., pp. 33–34. |
| 150 | "solemnity of communicants" | *The Doomsters*, p. 123. |
| 151 | "*Wall Street Journal*" | *The Galton Case*, p. 1. |
| 151 | "like being expelled" | Ibid. |
| 151 | "a small scale" | Macdonald, "Writing *The Galton Case*," p. 43. |
| 151 | "significance of this" | *The Galton Case*, p. 103. |
| 152 | "to be lost" | Ibid., p. 28. |

PAGE      QUOTE                          SOURCE

## Chapter 8

154-155 through extract   "for ocular    Geoffrey H. Hartman, *The Fate*
        proof"                           *of Reading and Other Essays*
                                         (Chicago: Univ. of Chicago Press,
                                         1975).

155     "without overrating it"         Thomas R. Edwards, "Tough
                                         Guys," *The New York Review of*
                                         *Books*, 30 September 1976, pp.
                                         13-15.

156     "light years ahead"             Richard O. Moore, "Ross Mac-
                                         donald," *The Writer in America*,
                                         p. 3.

156     "through its fiction"           Jon Carroll, "Ross Macdonald in
                                         Raw California," p. 149.

157     "novel of terror"               Leslie A. Fiedler, *Love and Death*
                                         *in the American Novel* (2nd ed.;
                                         New York: Dell Publishing Co.,
                                         1966), p. 6.

157     "of our minds"                  Ibid., p. 19.
157     "want to understand"            Richard O. Moore, *The Writer in*
                                         *America*, pp. 7-8.

157     "nothing is rereadable"         Hartman, p. 218.
158     "the ostensible meaning"        M. H. Abrams, *A Glossary of Lit-*
                                         *erary Terms*, (3rd ed.; New York:
                                         Holt, Rinehart and Winston,
                                         1971), p. 81.

158     "he means it"                   Ibid., p. 82.
158     "in my life"                    *The Zebra-Striped Hearse*, p. 7.
159     "conduct their lives"           Abrams, *A Glossary*, p. 102.
159     "the detective writers"         Somerset Maugham, as quoted
                                         by Raymond A. Sokolov, "The
                                         Art of Murder," p. 101.

159     "puzzles and smoking"           Edmund Wilson, as quoted by
                                         Raymond A. Sokolov, Ibid.

160     "knife is cutting"              *The Zebra-Striped Hearse*, p. 186.
160     "comes to birth"                Macdonald, "Writing *The Galton*
                                         *Case*," p. 33.

160     "by an American"                William Goldman, "The Finest
                                         Series of Detective Novels Ever
                                         Written by an American," *New*
                                         *York Times Book Review*, 1 June
                                         1969.

# Index

Abrams, M. H., 157-59
adolescence, 27
Algren, Nelson, 8
alienation, 126-35
    as basis of Macdonald's fiction, 126-42
    between human and natural forces, 97, 130
    *Blue Hammer* and, 127
    in California, 130
    causes of, 127-28
    *Dark Tunnel* and, 15, 127
    figurative language and, 144
    from the past, 20-22, 130-34
    from the world, 134-35
    *Galton Case* and, 52
    *Goodbye Look* and, 88
    *Three Roads* and, 20-22, 130-31
    *Trouble Follows Me* and, 16-17
    war and, 127-28
    women and, 129-30
    World War II and, 17
    *Zebra-Striped Hearse* and, 64
*American Adam, The* (Lewis), 125
American fiction:
    alienation and, 126
    civilization and, 126
    new start and, 125-26
Archer, Lew, 2, 5, 109-24
    adolescence of, 111-12

autobiographical statements and, 39
background of, 110
*Black Money* and, 82-85
blacks and, 33-34
*Blue Hammer* and, 104-108
*Chill* and, 67-78
contemporary world and, 10, 12
critiques of, 115-16
death and, 117
described, 109-24, 136
as a detective, 114-15
divorce of, 113-14
*Doomsters* and, 41-46
dreams of, 116-18
*Drowning Pool* and, 28-29
evil and, 64
exclusion of, in two novels, 34-36, 55
family of, 110-11
*Far Side of the Dollar* and, 82-85
*Find a Victim* and, 36
*Galton Case* and, 48-54
*Goodbye Look* and, 87-95
humanity of, 115-16, 122-23
humor of, 151-52
*Instant Enemy* and, 85-87
intensity of, 114
language and, 58-59
love and, 121-22

177